Virtual
Leadership

Virtual
Leadership

Learning to
lead differently

Ghislaine Caulat

with a Foreword
by Professor Mike Pedler

First published in 2012 by Libri Publishing

ISBN 978 1 907471 50 6

Design by Carnegie Publishing

Printed in the UK by Ashford Colour Press

Libri Publishing
Brunel House
Volunteer Way
Faringdon
Oxfordshire
SN7 7YR

Tel: +44 (0)845 873 3837

www.libripublishing.co.uk

Endorsements for
Virtual Leadership

Like many Managers of my generation, I learned to manage teams in the nineties. I learned to manage cross-functional teams in the first decade of the 21st century. This book was written for those of us willing to take the next step and tear down the barriers imposed by physical or geographical location in order to become virtual leaders in an ever increasing online workspace. The truths exposed in this book are not self evident. Relationships matter. Communication skills matter more than ever. A lot of the information presented in this book will seem counter-intuitive or 'different' to you. It will make you uneasy. It should. Managing effectively in an online world requires disciplines that many of us have yet to learn. I recommend that you start by reading this book.

Gerhard Peter Gross, President and CEO –
Mexico, Daimler Trucks North America LLC

Having just started work myself, I discovered that despite having grown up with social networking there is still much that this book can teach me about working in a virtual environment. I would highly recommend this book to anyone who wants to make the most of their skills in a virtual environment and help their colleagues to do the same.

Juliet Morgan, 'Digital Native'

This book opened my eyes to recognize the potential in virtual team work and communication. Some insights are real 'mindshifters' but the author takes you further and gives concrete, practical tools on how to improve a lot.

Per Norell, Manager Strategic HR, Seco Tools Group, Sweden

Contemporary research on Virtual Leadership – written about so succinctly with room for exploration for the reader. It is a joy to read such superb content, which I could relate to my own experience in today's ever growing virtual world. It is a tool kit for all generations and not only for Generation 'Y' to make you effective to deal with the realities of exercising Virtual Leadership. The book shifts Virtual Leadership from a popular catch phrase to the needs of today's ever growing digital, virtual world of Leadership. A must read for executives to leverage the full potential of technology available now and in future.

Vikrant Shrotriya, General Manager, Gulf, Novo Nordisk

In 2011, the author, Dr Ghislaine Caulat, was invited to DSM to run a couple of training workshops on effective virtual working. The training was a great success and has helped a lot on the most important elements of virtual working: how to listen, how we can trust and connect to everyone in the virtual group, how we can inspire a passion for our work, etc. In this book, you, the reader, will find more about the theories and findings that come from her research, as well as the key skills you need for virtual working and leadership in practice. It's a remarkable tool, with powerful tips in each chapter to power up your career. CEOs, managers, consultants, staff – all the people working in different areas, different countries, and with different cultural backgrounds will absolutely benefit from reading this book. The wisdom within will do wonders for your business. Finally, a personal remark: it is good to read it as a handbook, to read, practise, develop, read again and practise again…, connecting your world. Enjoy your journey.

Wei Tao, Affiliate Manager GTI China, DSM ICT

As a global NGO, working across 26 countries, we asked Dr Ghislaine Caulat to support us in building a network of internal virtual facilitators to sustain the work we have been doing around leadership development. We found the process extremely inspiring with the group gaining a range of new skills and approaches. The most important lesson was the recognition of how powerful 'virtual' is as a communication method, shattering the myth that face-to-face is always better. In this book, Ghislaine shares her insights, tips and theories around how to lead 'virtually', and makes these easily accessible and applicable to all leaders. I would encourage you to read, digest, and experiment with the approaches outlined – using them well will definitely deliver results.

Rachel Westcott, Director of People and Organisational Development, WaterAid

Contents

Contents

Figures

---

*   We are grateful to the Society for Organisational Learning, MIT Sloan School of Management, Cambridge, MA 02142, USA for their copyright permission to reproduce figure 6.

In the case of figure 5 we have been unable to trace any similar diagram, and would appreciate any information that would enable us to do so.

Acknowledgements

This book would not exist without the contribution of the leaders whom I have had the privilege to accompany for many years through the ups and downs of their virtual leadership. I would like to thank in particular William, Silvia, Barbara, Matthew and Sten as well as the many leaders from MilkCo. Although I mention them here in their disguised identities I know that they will recognise themselves: thank you for your dedicated cooperation, trust and openness to experimentation. It has been a really exciting and rewarding experience that will stay with me for the rest of my life.

I would like to thank the Digital Natives who contributed to this research: Julia, Katherine, Marion, Priscila, Pamela, Diego, Erika, Maya, Eilen and Sam. What a pleasure and sense of discovery to work and reflect with you all. Thank you for helping me to understand your world!

For me virtual leadership has become a journey of on-going learning and I would like to thank all the clients who have embarked on a virtual project with me. Thank you for your trust and the rich reflection that we have had so far and continue to have on a regular basis.

I also would like to thank Ina Smith, Dev Mookherjee and Duncan Smith from the then Leadership Team of Ashridge Consulting who have supported me, always with a word of encouragement and trusting me in the most unusual and daring plans. I also would like to express a huge thank you to my Doctoral supervisor Kathleen King for her dedication and care. Thank you also to the Doctoral Faculty and my peers for their helpful contribution and challenge.

Furthermore I would like to thank the colleagues at Ashridge who have been willing to take the challenge and embark with me on this virtual leadership work: thank you in particular to my ex-colleague Sally Hulks for having been such a wonderful partner in the very early hours of the work. Thank you to Sue Jabbar and Andy Copeland for their dedication, patience and endless efforts to continuously improve the quality of the learning experience that we offer to our clients in the virtual space.

Publishing this book has been in itself a virtual project. I would like to thank Paul Jervis of Libri Publishing for his flexibility and for agreeing to work virtually with me and for his ongoing guidance throughout the whole process. Last but not least thank you to my colleague Elizabeth Braiden for being such a good sparring partner and for her relentless checking of consistencies, with her amazing capability of combining the helicopter view with a sharp sense for details.

Foreword

There has been much talk of virtual teams and virtual leadership in the last 20 years, but perhaps much of this has been just talk. Just four years ago, together with colleagues, we initiated a research project on virtual action learning (VAL). At that time it felt like a distant frontier, and although we found it an exciting and inevitable idea we uncovered relatively few examples of practice. We thought that VAL was probably awaiting technological improvements and speculated about the use of virtual worlds such as Second Life.

Meanwhile Ghislaine Caulat was developing her highly innovative and personal practice by using the old technology of the telephone. By this trusty means she convenes action learning sets of people who have never met face-to-face, and promotes virtual collaboration between these erstwhile strangers with the help of some special focusing and connecting activities. Especially for those of us who are not sub-30 year old 'Digital Natives', virtual working might involve acquiring some new habits. Her practice involves teaching people how to focus – with meditative exercises – how to work with the silences, how to become aware of oneself, especially one's emotions, and how to take part in various online meeting rituals such as connecting and disconnecting.

These new habits and skills of virtual working may be surprisingly effective. Working alone and in a quiet space, whilst simultaneously being in attentive communication with others, may produce more productive outcomes than the busy and distracted face-to-face meetings to which we are more used.

This possibility allows the author to extend her action learning practice into a theory of virtual leadership. In her hands, the slightly fanciful idea discussed in our research becomes a practical tool for meeting, working and learning together. If it works for action learning then why should it not apply to all situations where people are geographically dispersed and must necessarily organise themselves for much of the time by remote communications?

In this view, virtual working is no reluctant necessity but a positively advantageous way of conducting business which allows for the best 'brains' to be deployed on the most demanding tasks wherever they are located, whilst at the same time greatly reducing the various costs and stresses involved in global organising – organisational, personal and environmental.

In perhaps the boldest claim in a generally bold book, this theory and practice of virtual leadership is further extended to propose a different way of thinking about leadership in general and in any setting. Paradoxically perhaps, the virtual environment promotes better leadership than the face-to-face (and taken-for-granted) situation, because the leader learns to put much of her effort into building and maintaining relationships. And because virtual leadership puts the emphasis on relationships and not just upon tasks, this in turn develops the leader as person in unexpected ways. The relational effort promotes a personal reflexivity and search for authenticity; to be a leader in this way you have to become more fully human. Or as Ken Wilber is quoted as saying in *Invitation 8: WHO are you?*: 'without interior development, healthy exterior development cannot be sustained'.

This reminds us that the search for personal integrity and the quest for self-development should be at the heart of management and leadership development. In recent years the double whammy of the celebrity CEO literature on the one hand, and the dehumanising search for competency modelling on the other, have obscured this essential vision. Neither the rehashing of charisma (in the interests of the publicist) nor the avoidance of the personal and the moral that emanate from conformance to models will help us much with the intractable organisational and social problems of our time. In this book leadership re-emerges as a personal and relational activity for every human being, and one which happens principally in the 'moments' of facilitation between us.

Doctoral studies do not often make good books. This is one of the exceptions, saved from the normally deferential nature of that pursuit by a lively and personal conviction, balanced by an openness and commitment to continuing inquiry. You don't have to accept all the claims made here to be taken with their creative potential and also with their essential warmth and sincerity.

Professor Mike Pedler
Hathersage
United Kingdom
25th September 2011

Who Is the Book For?

The book is primarily for leaders and managers in organisations responsible for people who cannot meet face-to-face or who do so only occasionally.

In the widest sense I have written this book for everybody involved in working and/or managing and/or leading virtually, and anybody wanting to help others to do so.

Unlike many other authors who have written on the topic of virtual working and virtual teams, I do not differentiate between so-called 'temporary virtual teams' (for example project teams whose members work on a specific task for a limited time, with a given start and end point) and organisational teams (for example whole departments, whose members happen to be located in different locations and hence need to work virtually, e.g. a global services team or a global HR team, a global communication team or a global research and development team). This means as a result that this book is targeting leaders or managers of virtual project teams (one could call them 'virtual project leaders' or 'virtual project managers') as well as leaders of departments that operate mainly or only virtually.

The reason why, eight years ago, I embarked on the research on virtual working and virtual teams was precisely that I wanted to understand why virtual working had remained unsatisfactory and why for most people it is second best, something that you do when you cannot travel and when you have no other alternative. Therefore this book is not only for leaders and managers who are about to start leading – and/or working with – a virtual team and do not know how and where to begin. It is also for those who have been working and leading virtually, possibly for many years, but who remain dissatisfied with their practice and want to find out how to make it more successful.

My aim throughout has been to write in such a way that the book would be practical to use. It is likely to appeal to people who appreciate hearing others' experiences, and learning by reflecting on these as a basis for experimenting with new ideas to improve their own practice.

People helping managers and leaders to work and lead virtually, for example Human Resources managers, so-called 'HR business partners', coaches, trainers and consultants (internal and external to the organisation) should also find helpful guidance and material here.

The book is written more for people working in organisations and less for people engaged in virtual open communities, for example using social media networks such as LinkedIn or Xing or Plaxo. While many aspects addressed here will also be relevant for these communities, the main discourse has not taken aspects of the latter into close consideration. This does not mean that I think that virtual open communities are not important. It only means that I decided to focus my research in order to offer in-depth, robust and practical insights to the question: 'What does it take to lead effectively a team of people working across geographies?'

A Reader's Guide

I would like to offer some guidance to anyone reading this book. Obviously everybody will read it as they wish. This might mean diving into specific parts, or starting from the end or starting from the first page and reading his/her way through to the last one (throughout the book, I usually include both male and female – if on any occasion I don't do so, please assume that both are included).

The book has been conceived in a specific way, actually in the hope that everybody can enter and exit it again in the manner they like. Nevertheless, I want to make my logic and intentions explicit, since this might provide helpful hints and tips to readers about how best they can make use of the time that they will dedicate to this work.

In the first chapter I explore why virtual working has remained such a challenge and, for most people so far, a dissatisfying practice. I also explain how I have developed my research and why I believe that this research – being different from previous approaches to the field of virtual working and leading – will offer different insights and new alternatives to the challenges in question.

Disguised identities

In the second chapter, I introduce my co-researchers, the virtual leaders who shared their journey to virtual leadership with me. I provide details about their backgrounds, their roles and challenges. I share the stories of their learning about virtual working and leading, as well as the story of my learning as a result. The majority of the names have been disguised, and in several instances organisational realities have been modified, to offer maximum anonymity to my co-researchers.

Nevertheless, the stories and the outcomes are all true in as much as I have made sense of what we (my co-researchers and I) were learning and cross-checked this with them as we were progressing in our reflections. As to the key 'protagonists' of the research (William, Silvia, Sten, Matthew, and

Barbara) they all had the opportunity to read and to agree to what I have written about them.

I also introduce MilkCo, a global organisation with whom I have worked virtually on a major strategy project. I refer to this assignment throughout the text since it occurs at the junction of my research and my consulting, and offers a wealth of useful insights.

Eight invitations on eight key aspects of virtual leadership
The core of the book consists of eight 'invitations' to my readers. Each of these deals with a specific aspect of working and leading virtually.

Each invitation starts with the claim which I am making in relation to that specific aspect, and relates to one or more stories and examples from which I have deduced the learning and upon which I am basing the claim. More importantly, the stories are there for readers to test their resonance with their own experiences, as a way of checking the validity of these claims for themselves.

Where relevant, some academic material is provided as a way to further support the claims (some of which might feel rather counter-intuitive and challenging). However this material has been provided in a specific and distinctively different format so that any reader has the freedom to decide whether to read or to skip it and move on to further stories.

In the same vein, readers interested in understanding or knowing more about the concepts which I mention, either in terms of philosophy or methodology, can find more in the **glossary** at the end of the book. In this I provide more information about the key concepts which I introduce in the different chapters of the book.

'So what?'...and letting the stories speak to you
At the end of each invitation, you, the reader, will find a 'so what?' section. My aim in so doing is to guide you in your reflection, and invite you to remember a minimum of key points which you can apply in your own virtual working and leadership practice. As I am keen to offer this book as a practical – albeit in-depth reflexive – book for busy leaders 'out there' who need succinct and concrete help, I felt it was imperative to offer this 'so what?' section for each invitation. Nevertheless, this has been an interesting challenge for me: while appreciating the value of concise opinions I find that bullet point summaries can be unhelpful in the sense that they reduce juicy stories to a few points which might prove difficult to apply to the diversity of real organisational life.

Hence my 'so what?' summaries are more intended to help readers to remember the key points on which to practise, but they are not intended to be definitive statements, either conclusive or exhaustive ones. I prefer to let the stories speak for themselves and invite readers to make sense for themselves of what they read, and draw their own conclusions based on whether the real-life stories resonate with them or not, and whether they are moved by the stories or not.

Therefore, my hope is that you will read through the invitation of your choice, from the beginning to the end and that the 'greyed-out' parts, namely the claim at the start and the 'so what?' section at the end will provide a useful reminder for your practice – in addition to any notes that you might have made for yourself when reading through.

Invitations as 'stand-alone'

Each invitation is like an invitation to you, the reader, to try out a specific approach. I am inviting you to experiment with the invitations that make most sense to you and to adapt and modify your practice accordingly, based on what you find most compelling and helpful.

Hence this book is not meant as a recipe or as an all-encompassing methodology to succeed in the virtual space. It is more a series of invitations to experiment with different approaches, reflect on and learn from them. Therefore each invitation can be read and re-read on a 'stand-alone' basis, which I hope will make the book even more practical and helpful. A consequence of this is that, in some instances – which I have endeavoured to keep to a minimum – some key aspects will be repeated across the invitations. When repetitions would have been too heavy, I have sign-posted links between invitations, but I have tried to do this in such a way that the text in each invitation is self-sufficient, and readers do not have to read the other invitations associated with the one they are reading, if they choose not to.

A tool box

In support of the invitations, readers will find a 'tool box' at the end of the book. In this they will find a carefully selected number of 'tools' or devices such as frameworks or lists of questions on which to reflect, etc. My hope is that these might provide further practical help in some specific instances related to the challenges described.

Again, as in a real 'tool box', the aim is not to use all frameworks and devices as a recipe or method to solve a problem. The purpose is much more for the reader to choose the ones which might be helpful and make most sense to them, in a 'pick and mix' fashion.

Finally a last invitation: come and share with me!

Over the years, I have become clearer and clearer that virtual leadership is a new discipline which deserves to be researched from the idiosyncrasies of the virtual paradigm (as opposed to reducing the learning to the traditional – primarily face-to-face based – paradigm of leadership). As a consequence, virtual leadership also needs *to be learnt* as a new discipline – which is precisely what this book is about.

My sense is that we are only just entering this new territory and that we have only just begun to sketch out the map for its exploration. Virtual leadership is and will be ongoing learner-ship for very many years to come. My own learning has been growing from client to client, from challenge to challenge, from organisation to organisation. Sharing this learning is a powerful undertaking, which again is why I have decided to share these stories as opposed to presenting recipes for success.

My big hope is that readers of this book will also be willing and keen to carry on the journey, and share their stories with further readers and (to be) virtual leaders. For those wishing to do so, the necessary access details to my website are provided in 'Final considerations' at the end of this book.

CHAPTER 1:
Stories Instead of Recipes

Why Has Virtual Working Remained So Difficult?
I have reflected often on the questions:
- Why do so many people reject or dislike virtual working?

- Why do they struggle with it?

Is it because it is inherently incompatible with human nature, or is it only a question of time? Will people get used to it and adopt this new way of working and communicating, just as they adopted the use of cars or microwaves decades ago? Are we just considering patterns in the adoption of a new technology? This curiosity led me to undertake substantial, practical research into what needs to happen for virtual working and leadership to be truly successful. In this book I present my key findings.

Like it or not, virtual working has become essential in the last few years, prompted by ever-increasing globalisation, a growing care for the environment, a concern for a better quality of life, the need to cut costs and the desire to welcome into the corporate world Generation Y (people born in the 1980s who have grown up with all today's virtual media).

Virtual working truly is nothing new though. This way of working (mediated by communication technology) has been practised for at least twenty years, and a great deal has been written about the topic. But even after so many years, virtual working remains an unsatisfactory practice which at best is considered as 'second class'; something you do when you cannot travel.

For most people, virtual working is associated with something that is not real or is superficial. For the vast majority of managers I have come across in organisations, personal contact can only equate to face-to-face contact. I am constantly amazed when people say to each other: 'I look forward to meeting you personally' when they mean 'meeting you face-to-face', even though they have already been working together virtually for perhaps six months. I wonder what they have been doing all this time. Have they not developed some sense of each other at a personal level? If not, why is it like that?

Several stories of abusive relationships developing on the internet and reported by the media have not helped to create a positive openness about virtual communication, at least for the sceptical among us. Nor has the flurry of books with recipes and 'how to' lists about virtual working really helped to overcome the hurdles and apprehension. 'Virtual' in many people's heads still remains something superficial, and linked with technology which therefore can be only of limited benefit in the workplace.

The interesting thing, however, is that the word 'virtual' is an old word, first appearing in the late 14th century and meaning: 'influencing by physical virtues or capabilities', from *virtualis*, and *virtus* 'excellence, potency, efficacy".* In the mid 17th century the word's semantic field expanded and incorporated the idea of 'essence'.

One main reason that virtual working has remained unsatisfactory is that the leadership aspect of this work has been underestimated, if not completely forgotten. Most literature speaks about 'managing virtual teams' and focuses on the tasks at hand and the things to do and not do. My research shows that leading virtually represents a new discipline, different from traditional leadership, one that needs to be recognised as such and learnt.

Over the last ten years and more the issue of virtual working in organisations has kept many minds busy. First the opinion was that, if one ensured that the right technology was in place, virtual working would be efficient; next the literature focused more on getting the right team and the right processes in place in order to ensure effective virtual working. This line of thinking has been developed further, and has led to an impressive number of what I call 'recipe books' about virtual working and virtual teams. In the last five years more literature has been published about trust and managing performance in the virtual world. The focus on *virtual leadership* as opposed to *managing virtual teams* remains, nevertheless, very limited.

The findings from my research show that the teams which perform best are the ones whose members learn to work in the virtual space on the relationship aspects, as well as on the task, and who become independent of the need to meet face-to-face. In contrast, the teams which focus only on the task and the management aspects of it, plateau at some point and remain dependent on the face-to-face to reach new levels of performance. While the high-performing virtual teams recognise the need for leadership in the virtual space, the ones who plateau in their performance keep focusing on the management aspects of virtual working.

My inquiry into what it takes to lead effectively virtually actually revisits the original sense of the word 'virtual'. It shows that, paradoxically, by

---

* *Online Etymology Dictionary*, © 2010 Douglas Harper

To develop high performing virtual teams it is necessary to focus on the relationship AS MUCH AS on the task

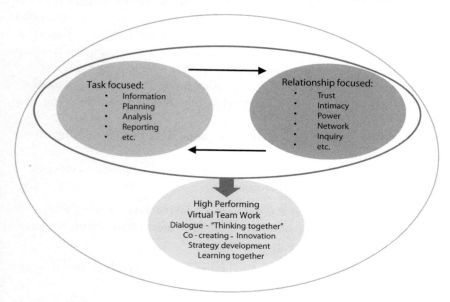

Figure 1: Relationship focus and task focus worked on together

learning to lead well virtually, leaders become better leaders than they were before, becoming more anchored in the awareness of their being as leaders of and to others. It is as if they become more aware of their 'virtue' and 'essence' as a result, or as if they become more 'real' in their presence and their quality as leaders.

In the process of learning to become effective virtual leaders, they need to go to a deeper level of reflection, and question key aspects such as their own sense of identity as leaders, their relationships, and issues of trust and power. In so doing, they realise that some of their practices actually become questionable in their traditional leadership activities as well. By learning to lead virtually, the leaders I have worked with have learnt to become better and more 'real' leaders.

If teams recognise that achieving high performance in the virtual space requires true leadership, and if leaders understand that leading in the virtual space is a new discipline that needs to be recognised in its own right and learnt with all the competences and skills it entails, then most barriers will disappear.

In the context of my practice, I now come across a slowly but surely increasing number of organisations which have recognised the power of effective virtual working, and trust virtual teams with highly demanding assignments. This could be, for example, a global services department whose members are scattered across four continents and serve their internal customers around the globe and the clock in the most effective way. Or it could be that a senior management team dispersed across countries is tasked with the development of a new strategy, or that a temporary team working across continents is tasked with developing innovative approaches for their organisation when it comes to entering new markets or developing new services or products.

All these examples show that, when done well, virtual working allows organisations to:

- use their best brains for the most demanding assignments independently of geographical locations

- develop strategies that are closer to local markets, by being able to involve managers from all their affiliates more often and on a regular basis into their strategy meetings

- avoid the financial, environmental and personal costs related to moving people around

- increase the quality of life for their managers (at least for those who no longer consider travelling so exciting) by enabling them to work more from home, and to spend less time on aeroplanes and hanging around airports or train stations.

Understanding what it takes to lead effectively virtually, and learning to do this well is key to unlocking the real potential of the virtual space and achieving real competitive advantage in today's economies.

A different book

Before engaging in this research, and throughout it, I kept asking myself: 'What is the difference that will make a difference? What can I do differently in terms of my research approach, and the way I present it, so that the results help leaders to make a real shift in the way they perceive and practice virtual working and leading?'

I decided to share the stories of my co-researchers, the leaders whom I had the privilege of accompanying over the years. Now I explore and reflect on these stories, together with my experience with a range of clients working virtually. From these reflections, I formulate eight 'invitations' which seem to my co-researchers, clients and me, to encapsulate the most critical aspects of virtual leadership practice.

I would like to offer to readers these invitations as suggestions with which they can experiment and learn for their virtual leadership practice.

I have chosen to offer this emerging knowledge to leaders aiming to lead in the virtual space in the form of 'invitations' as opposed to a set of models or frameworks. This choice was informed specifically by the social constructionist principles (see glossary). The social constructionist view claims that there is not one objective truth but that the meaning of reality is constantly created among ourselves, and that we have no choice but to create meaning, which requires making choices together (Gergen 1999). The aim of my research has not been to reach final results in the form of 'knowing that' or 'knowing how', but rather to offer words as 'joint action' (Shotter 1993b), as a way to engage with my readers.

Shotter (1993) sees managers as 'practical authors': managers are not about applying management theories, they are about formulating and creating conditions within which they offer 'intelligible formulations' (Shotter 1993, p.148) of issues or happenings that first appear to others as chaotic and complex. In so doing they become 'authors' of realities and enable others to act on them. I find this an exciting view of leadership and followership, and have been wondering how this 'authoring' would look in the virtual space, as it might be even more relevant there than in traditional leadership contexts because of the lack of points of reference, hence the increased degree of complexity. Through my own attempt to practise 'practical authoring' I have not only endeavoured to **research** in a way that is informed by a social constructionist perspective, but at the same time I have strived to **lead** my leaders-readers into this unknown territory in 'practical authoring' fashion.

The virtual leader that you will become

I hope that the concrete lived examples of my co-inquirers as well as mine will be useful examples with which my readers can associate or recognise from their own virtual leadership experience. Hence the 'invitations' I offer in this book, accompanied with a series of questions and / or guidance, are intended to help the reader to reflect and to work on 'the virtual leader that I will become', as opposed to becoming the virtual leader that I, the researcher, advise that s/he should become.

CHAPTER 2:
Research *With* Virtual Leaders *For* Virtual Leaders

I am not stating anything new by saying that much is written about leadership. There are as many definitions as there are potential researchers. Furthermore, as touched on earlier, it seems that the considerable number of books about virtual working and virtual teams have not really contributed to changing significantly the situation around virtual working.

I decided to undertake research into virtual leadership. So – where to start? While I agreed with Zhang and Fjermestad (2006) about the paucity of theoretical rigour in virtual leadership studies, I had some reservations about engaging in research that would narrow the outcomes too quickly to well-known theoretical models about leadership (which is what both authors do and advocate that others should do). This reservation was prompted by two concerns. Firstly, as mentioned already, researchers cannot seem to agree on what leadership is about, so how would I go about choosing one or a number of frameworks for my research? Secondly, my biggest concern was that by reducing my questions and approach to fit within the current thinking, developed from within a predominantly face-to-face paradigm, I might be doing something incongruent with the very topic of my research about virtual leadership, and might close a door to new, emerging learning before having even tried to open it.

I decided to carry out a four-year long research project, accompanying real leaders who needed (to learn how) to lead virtually. I was privileged enough to accompany them on the ups and downs of their journey, to reflect and learn with them about what it actually takes to lead well virtually and what it takes to develop a virtual team into a high performing one. In doing so I could gather a good number of stories and examples, real stories from real leaders leading real teams virtually.

I engaged in a quest to interpret my findings (all the stories and examples) through robust theoretical thinking about leadership while remaining open and true to my topic. I was inspired by the phenomenological perspective (see glossary) described by Ladkin in *Rethinking Leadership* (2010).

Rather than attempting to provide yet another definition of leadership, Donna Ladkin, Senior Lecturer at Cranfield School of Management in the UK, challenges the very questions and answers given by so many researchers about leadership. Instead of answering the question 'What is leadership?' she takes a more philosophical perspective and inquires into the actual phenomenon of leadership. The majority of Western-based leadership theories are derived from research methods based on a positivistic approach: in the same way as one would research on physics, a majority of leadership researchers break down leadership into several characteristics such as competencies and traits. As a consequence a series of psychometric tools have been conceived to measure and develop these characteristics in leaders. Ladkin takes the post-positivist approach, and offers distinctive insights about leadership by revisiting the questions asked about leadership and inquiring into the phenomenon of leadership itself.

I summarise below the key reasons why I found this perspective helpful in the context of what I was trying to achieve:

1) Phenomenology encourages us to look at leadership as a phenomenon (and not for example, as the personal traits of a leader or as a fixed process) and to consider this phenomenon in close connection with the context in which it develops.

2) Attending to the particular circumstances in which virtual leadership arises, as opposed to an abstract theoretical framework – or even worse, one informed by a face-to-face paradigm of thought – seems to me to be absolutely critical in order to do justice to a different and virtual space in which leadership might emerge.

3) The stance of 'living the questions' advocated by Ladkin, as opposed to searching for answers and definitions, appears to me to be fully congruent with the Action Research methodology (see glossary) that I have chosen for this work. In practical terms this means that in my research I have put the emphasis on exploring and describing **real life examples of what it takes to lead virtually**, and have dedicated considerable effort to reflecting on these, instead of urging myself to come to conclusions. In other words I have chosen both to start and to work from real life examples from the world of real virtual leaders, and to hold myself in the process of making sense for an extended period of time, as opposed to starting from some hypotheses that I would have sought to verify in practice.

4) I feel particularly attracted by the concept of 'moments' of leadership. Ladkin emphasises that this is not a time-related concept, but a concept encouraging us to look at leadership as a phenomenon fully dependent on other phenomena, such as the organisation in which it happens, the people working together, the intention of the researcher (i.e. for what purpose does s/he do the research on leadership: To help the academic world? To help leaders improve their effectiveness? etc.):

> "[...] leadership cannot exist apart from the particular individuals who are engaged and involved in any leadership dynamic. Leadership does not exist without people who are in some way identified as 'leaders' and people who are identified as people they will lead. Neither can it exist outside a particular community or organisational culture or history. For these reasons I argue that rather than being a 'whole', leadership can best be described as a 'moment' of social relations. What does this imply about how we might come to understand leadership? Recognizing leadership as a 'moment' suggests that we can never arrive at the reality of leadership as separated from those particular contexts in which it arises". (Ladkin 2010)

I am fully aware of the weight of this last sentence in terms of the implications that it might have for my research and the results that I share in this book. All the way through I have been asking myself: 'How useful is my research going to be for the leaders for whom I am writing it?'

The approach I have selected means that what I can aspire to is the description and reflection of lived and concrete 'moments' of virtual leadership with real leaders in the real world, combined with intense reflection and 'living the question' of what it takes to lead virtually. What I cannot (and do not want to) aspire to is the delivery of a new leadership model at the end. Having said that, my aim has been to select a wide and diverse range of leadership 'moments' in different contexts and with different people, in the hope that my readers will be able to identify themselves with some aspects of these. Furthermore, although I have decided to remain open for as long as possible in my research, I have also been able to identify common patterns across my inquiry strands with strong implications for virtual leadership. I anticipate (and hope) that these might serve as useful guidance for virtual leaders in their own leadership 'moments'.

I would now like to introduce my co-researchers, the virtual leaders who shared their journey to virtual leadership with me.

Working with William, Silvia and Sten

(In order to protect the identity of my co-researchers I have changed their names and those of their companies. I do so with all managers and companies throughout this book.)

William is a Belgian manager at a senior level in CompCorp. He has led teams (approximately 1,500 people in total) over six plants in Belgium and Sweden in a blend of face-to-face and virtual work for the last three years. I got to know William during a leadership development programme which was run by Ashridge Consulting. I soon developed a strong respect for William, in particular for his attitude, which I felt was open, thoughtful and engaging. During the time that I worked with him, William had to overcome extremely challenging situations in terms of management and leadership, and the need for him to lead virtually became ever more critical.

Sten is British and works for a multinational process engineering company. At the time of my research Sten was in charge of a particular market segment in the Nordic and Baltic countries and the UK. He was responsible for a virtual team including five direct reports based in different countries and another seven indirect reports in other countries. He was based in the UK while his boss was based in Finland. I had known Sten for at least ten years. I got to know him when I was working at RolloCorp and we did a lot of work together. Sten and I got on well and, as with William, I have always appreciated his openness. My work with Sten stopped earlier than that with William and Silvia because, after about a year, Sten changed his role to local Sales Director, still within the same organisation, but without the regular need to work virtually.

Silvia represents a different case. I have never met her face-to-face. I only got to know her within the context of my research. She was recommended by a friend and immediately agreed to participate in the research. Silvia is German and works in Sweden for a global telecommunication company: she leads a team across the world (Japan, China, Korea, US, Brazil, Mexico, Hungary and Sweden). Silvia's is a typical matrix-based team, which means that she has no direct reports. At the time I started working with Silvia the team had met face-to-face only twice in three years.

I contracted carefully about the work that we would do. I had a briefing and contracting session with each of the leaders upfront, and agreed how we would work together.

With Sten I had a total of four conversations of approximately two hours each, two of which were face-to-face. The conversations were taped. I also took notes, reflected on each conversation, and brought my own insights from the conversation to the next one to check with Sten his insights, experiences and reflections as an ongoing cycle of inquiry. I also followed up on the actions that he decided to take and heard from him what he learnt.

With Silvia and William I had an average of one conversation every three months, with a total of twelve conversations of between two to three hours each. My plans had to be modified as a consequence of a reduction in the time that Silvia and William could give to the work with me. All conversations were on the phone. As with Sten, I followed up on the actions that they had planned to take and helped them summarise their learning; I engaged in an ongoing inquiry, checking my insights with them and asking them for their insights and any new questions emerging from the process.

Collaborative inquiry with Matthew, Barbara and Silvia

I found my research with the three leaders I was accompanying very rich. However, at times I felt that the one-to-one exchanges, where my co-researcher and I were trying to make sense of what was happening, could benefit from a wider circle of people to reflect with. Hence I decided to initiate a collaborative inquiry (see glossary) in addition to the other strands of inquiry. Some way into my research, I organised and facilitated a collaborative inquiry with three virtual leaders, all based in different organisations. This proved to be a very rewarding and rich experience as well.

The people engaged in this inquiry were:

Matthew, who was working globally as an accounting director for an IT company

Barbara, the CEO of an NGO working across geographical zones including India, Africa and the UK

Silvia, who was mentioned earlier as one of the leaders I had been accompanying over the previous two years on a one-to-one basis.

None of the three inquirers knew each other before our work together and they did not meet face-to-face during the process. As mentioned, I never met Silvia face-to-face but I had been working with her for two years when we started the inquiry. I had met Matthew in the context of a Global Leadership programme that I ran for his organisation a few years earlier, and I met Barbara in the context of some consulting work that I happened to do for her organisation seven years earlier. In order to create an environment in which all of us would feel comfortable and safe, I paid a lot of attention to bringing people together whose organisations were not competing with each other and who had practised the art of leading virtually for some while. One thing that I had neither planned for nor designed into the process, but which soon turned out to be a strong common denominator for all three inquirers, was that they all had to lead virtually teams or members of teams based in India.

In terms of methodology, I used a collaborative inquiry approach that I will describe below.

The sessions we had were held over a period of seven months as represented in the following figure:

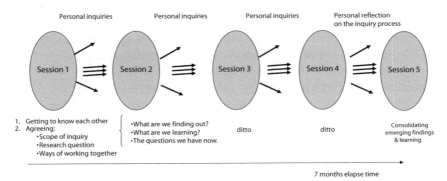

Figure 2: The process of our collaborative inquiry group

We discussed in detail how each of us wanted to go about inquiring into our virtual leadership. I suggested some kind of collective discussion format during the sessions. In addition, to support individuals in their personal inquiries, I suggested journal-keeping between the sessions, to assist us in reflecting on our ongoing virtual leadership. Silvia said from the beginning that she was not keen on journal-keeping, although Barbara was. Matthew seemed unclear as to the way he wanted to reflect between the sessions (our virtual meetings). During the sessions we ended up at times using a format of exploration similar to an action learning format, while at other times we would end up having an open dialogue about the specific aspects that we were noticing. I was not attached to any specific format of exchange and reflection, so we let the conversations emerge. At the end of each session I would invite the group to check whether the format we had chosen was helpful for our learning and/or whether we should amend it for the next session. The only element to which I was personally attached was to explore not only our respective virtual leadership but also our experience of virtual leadership in the very group that we were forming. My co-researchers agreed to this.

A final point regarding the method was that we agreed that I would record our sessions – which we held on a web-based platform, WebEx, and that I would send the recording to everyone after each session.

The MilkCo inquiry

At much the same time, two Ashridge colleagues and I had the opportunity to work on an exciting virtual project with a Scandinavian company, MilkCo, in the chemical industry (the name of the company is fictitious and several parameters have been modified to ensure anonymity). The three of us knew MilkCo pretty well because we had worked with the organisation before. At the outset, my colleague Peter (client director for MilkCo) came to me and explained the client's request: they wanted to work on one of the most critical strategic questions for the organisation and to involve their top management worldwide; in addition they had only a very limited time to do so (four months). My immediate reaction was to suggest a virtual process. As my colleague Peter had always been very open and supportive of the virtual approach, it didn't take me long to convince him.

Together we designed a virtual approach that was presented to the client, who immediately accepted it. The work that I will now describe as a 'virtual strategy process' involved 48 MilkCo top executives from around the world (including Korea, India, China, Malaysia, Argentina, Brazil, the US and Europe) as well as several members of the Board, including the CEO who took an active part in the final virtual conference involving a total of 55 people. The sponsor of the project was a member of the Board and played an important role in the process.

The work started with a two-day face-to-face workshop at Ashridge during which the managers were introduced to the initiative, the rationale behind it and its purpose. They were also exposed to some external provocation linked to the strategic question on which they had to work: several leaders from other organisations as well as a few academics came to present on a specific aspect linked to the strategic challenge in question. At the end of the workshop the MilkCo executives were organised into five project teams that would work on different yet interrelated aspects. Each team had five or six members and was coached by one of three of us from Ashridge. Peter coached one team, Lee, another colleague, coached two teams, and I also coached two teams. From then on all work was done virtually, using a web-based platform as well as teleconferences.

My Ashridge colleagues and I coached the teams during five of their virtual meetings on WebEx. We had paid a lot of attention to the way we would position and deliver the coaching. Our aim was to support the team to deliver best performance within a very short amount of time: this would include helping the team with the actual content of their project where appropriate and needed. The coaching was principally though to help each team to develop effective ways of working virtually together.

We discussed comprehensively what this might involve and agreed that a minimum would be that at the start of each virtual meeting the coach would work with the team to enable them to connect well at a relationship level before jumping to the task. After that the team would be left to their own devices to do the work in the way they wanted. The coach would simply observe virtually. Sometimes, if so contracted with the team, the coach might interrupt the process and ask a question to help them to become aware of what was going on at a process level. Only at the end of the meeting would the coach take back the facilitation role and enable the team to reflect on what they had achieved, how they felt they had worked together, and what they had learnt. The coach would offer some feedback, raise questions and give advice when appropriate based on what s/he had observed.

My colleagues and I came together virtually on a regular basis and reflected on how our respective team(s) were doing, how the overall process was going, how our role was helping, etc. We were genuinely concerned to add value and give helpful support to teams, who were working under high pressure in a virtual space, so we kept checking with each other as to what coaching in the virtual space meant and whether we were serving our clients' needs as well as possible.

In addition we planned three cross-project team workshops as part of the process. One representative from each team would attend these workshops to present the current status of work within their team and to discuss with his/her counterparts possible overlaps and/or synergies between the teams, as well as the emerging questions regarding the strategic initiative. I facilitated these workshops with Lee and Peter. The project sponsor of MilkCo took an active and very helpful part in guiding and supporting the teams. At the end of the process (after four months of intense work) all teams came together with seven members of the Board of MilkCo and other MilkCo employees, discussed the outcomes of the project work and made decisions about the implementation of the outcomes based on an analysis of implications and prioritisation. All this took place in a virtual conference which I facilitated with my two colleagues.

The whole virtual process had been a very intense and rewarding experience for all parties involved – not only was the client very satisfied with the process and its outcomes, but the Ashridge team felt happy about it too. In agreement with the MilkCo project sponsor and my colleague Peter, I embarked on a series of interviews with the participants. I wanted to explore their experience in more depth and inquire with them into what they felt and thought it took for a leader to lead virtually, based on their experience of this virtual strategy process.

I carried out twenty one-to-one phone interviews, their duration varying between 45 and 75 minutes. My interviewees had been invited from across the teams and had accepted the interview on a voluntary basis. I had invited 21 people and 20 had accepted the invitation spontaneously. I believe that they were representative of the whole group because they belonged to different teams and had very different cultural and functional backgrounds. I chose not to record the interviews. Instead, I took notes on what I heard and, in the course of the conversation, checked my understanding. I had also assured my interviewees that their contributions would be anonymised, in the sense that the reader could not attribute their examples and opinions to any person in particular.

Most of my questions were open and clearly linked to the concrete experience of the interviewees within the context of the 'virtual strategy process'. I was keen to focus on the experience of leading and/or being led virtually, and on the specific 'moments of leadership' (Ladkin 2010). With each interviewee I took great care upfront to make sure that they understood that I was not seeking feedback regarding how Ashridge had led the process. I also assured them that there were no right or wrong answers to my questions, rather I was genuinely and only interested in their personal experience of the virtual process.

Doctoral workshop and the subsequent inquiry

In the context of the doctoral programme (that I completed at Ashridge), all participants were asked to facilitate a workshop in their field of research. For me this represented an excellent opportunity to inquire into my topic (Virtual Leadership) with peers who were keen to explore and reflect. My previous experience with clients led me to expect that the majority were likely to be, at best, rather sceptical, and possibly even negative about how much one can achieve in the virtual space. However, the same experience also meant that I expected them to be more open and positive after their first experience of a virtual event in a group. I therefore decided to put the emphasis on experiential learning in the first instance. I was keen to test my emerging findings with my peers in the light of what they would experience with me in the virtual space.

The workshop turned out to be a rich, intense and emotional event; not only the first day, which happened virtually, but also the second day in the traditional face-to-face setting at Ashridge. Several peers mentioned afterwards that my workshop had contributed to helping the group to move to another level of awareness about itself and to find a language to speak about itself that it had not used before. The workshop also generated several highly interesting questions related to the way people generally connect and engage with each other. The virtual experience had provided a platform from which my peers and I could look into our usual ways of connecting through a different lens, maybe even with a fresh eye.

After the workshop I had several one-to-one conversations with peers who were willing to reflect with me on the workshop, and who confirmed the significance of the event for our group. I was keen to write a paper and to offer it to my peers as a way to further engage in the inquiry; in other words I wanted to go into a second loop of inquiry with my peers. In order to help the reader understand my inquiry process around the workshop I have represented the different inquiry loops in the following figure:

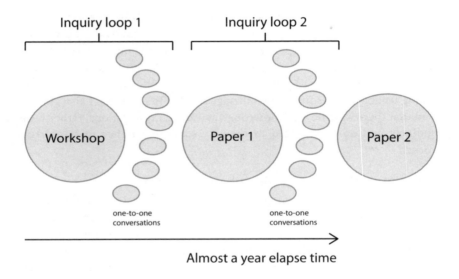

Figure 3: Inquiry loops – Doctoral workshop

The relevance of the Doctoral workshop for my research

This workshop had given me the opportunity to inquire into the details of the interactions between peers and faculty in the virtual environment. It was a privileged opportunity to 'take our experience seriously' (Stacey and Griffin 2005) with people striving for good inquiry work. I also believe that the doctoral community can to some extent be taken as a microcosm of organisations with all the organising patterns implied. I therefore hope that the emerging learning is relevant not only for my doctoral peers, faculty and myself but also for my readers.

Based on my research so far, I think that I can claim that this workshop gave me the opportunity to start inquiring into virtual leadership at the micro and/or local level of personal relationships and interactions in a way that has not been done before.

> Panteli and Chiasson echo these different levels in their research about virtual working:
>
> *"It follows that to view virtuality as being merely a global phenomenon provides us with only a partial understanding of its impact and pervasiveness. Virtuality is also a local phenomenon that needs to be examined from micro-level analysis as well as macro-level analysis".* (Panteli et al 2008, p.2)
>
> The authors underline that virtual interactions are still realised in the particular setting of individuals, and this influences the way virtual systems are used and managed.
>
> Hine explains how people have used extreme examples of the Internet, and sees this as unhelpful; instead she also pleads for a real effort to understand local phenomena of the Internet:
>
> *"To date, far more effort has been expended on predicting the revolutionary futures of the Internet than has been put into finding out in detail how it is being used and the ways in which it is being incorporated into people's daily lives".* (Hine 2000)

The 'Digital Natives'

In the context of my inquiry I returned on a number of occasions to the question 'is the reluctance by many people to engage in virtual working simply a symptom of the difficulty experienced in adapting to any new technology?' How many times, for example, have I been at a railway station and observed young people around me standing in a small circle, and instead of talking to each other frantically busy sending SMS to other friends? How many times have I heard from friends that they are worried about their son or daughter who spends hours in front of the computer either playing games in cyberspace or communicating with friends on Facebook?

Whether we like it or not, whether we are sceptical or not, some of us are currently spending a substantial amount of time in virtual waters and we particularly need to acknowledge that the younger generation have grown up in a world where virtual spaces such as Second Life or Facebook have become a natural part of their lives, in the same way that television became a natural part of our parents' and/or our generation's. Marc Prensky has coined the term 'Digital Natives' (2001) to describe this new generation. He was followed by others such as Rymaszweski et al (2007). What may be considered by us as virtual global weird stuff represents normal activity to the 'Digital Natives'.

All these considerations led me to think that maybe the next generation, being already used to virtual communication, will not face the same doubt or struggle as their parents when it comes to working virtually with others. So maybe my question about what makes effective virtual leadership (and implicitly why it seems to be so difficult) is only relevant for certain generations. In agreement with Hine (2000) I wanted actually to analyse and research how young people currently connect virtually. I was therefore keen to move beyond what I observed and heard. I decided to do some research with young people to better understand how they currently use virtual ways of communicating, how they are with others virtually, how they currently look at their professional future and what role virtual communication would play in this. I hoped that this would give me further insights regarding the topic of virtual leadership.

My interviews with 'Digital Natives'

I tried to speak with a fairly wide range of people who were not already too engaged in their professional careers and at the same time who would be old and mature enough to have some experience of communicating virtually and have the willingness to reflect about it.

My interviewees were an international mix of cultures and genders, although there was a majority of female interviewees. I performed the following interviews:

- A one-to-one conversation with Marion, an Anglo-French lady (22 years old) living in the UK who had just finished studying geography and started a job with an international company.

- A teleconference with Julia and Katherine, both 18-year-old British girls who had just finished school with excellent A level results in the summer and were about to start their studies, in chemistry (for Julia) and veterinary surgery (for Katherine).

- A teleconference with Priscila, Pamela, Diego and Erika. All four are Brazilians. Priscila (27 years old) lives in Barcelona, has completed her studies of cinema and has just started to work on the production of films. Pamela is 22 years old and is studying interpretation and translation of languages (Portuguese, English and German) in Heidelberg (Germany), Erika is 20 years old and studying biology in Brazil together with Diego, who is 21 years old.

- A teleconference with Maya, Elien and Sam. All three are Belgian youngsters. Maya is 16 years old and attends High School; she is learning Greek and Latin and loves music. Elien is a friend of Maya, also 16 years old and at the same school as Maya. She is learning modern languages (Dutch, French, English and German) and is also a musician. Sam is a 17-year-old boy who is studying informatics, knows a lot about computer communication technologies and plays several musical instruments. When we had the teleconference it was the first time that Elien had talked to Sam as they had no prior knowledge of each other.

Although none of the interviewees apart from Julia knew me face-to-face, all phone conversations ended up being spontaneous, open and very enjoyable. I was actually pleasantly surprised by how quickly my interviewees seemed to connect with me and I with them, and in how much depth we managed at times to discuss some topics.

One of the interviewees, Maya, observed at the end of the teleconference with Sam, Elien and myself:

> "It is really surprising how fast you can have a detailed conversation with very personal views of people on a specific subject, even when you have no idea about the rest of their lives".

It turned out that none of my interviewees was used to having phone conversations with more than one person (their ways of communication include media such as SMS, Facebook, etc) and I was surprised by how naturally and fast they got on with it. At the end of the conversation with Maya, Elien and Sam I asked how they had experienced it, given that Sam didn't know Elien before. The two of them said that they initially thought that it would be very weird and that they had concerns that the conversation would be boring and technical, and that they actually found that 'As we started it all went great and it was very OK' as Elien put it.

Examples from my practice

Finally, in this book, I will also be sharing examples from my consulting practice. While the MilkCo inquiry represents an example at the intersection between my work and my research, there are many more examples with many other organisations with which I have done intense work over the last seven years. In particular, I have helped their leaders to develop their competence to lead virtually and to learn virtually over the years. This work has all been delivered in the virtual space and has given me a very rich source of examples to learn from, and to draw on in sharing my findings.

INVITATION 1
Virtual Leaders Need To Learn, Relearn And Unlearn

With this invitation, I describe how the virtual leader needs to recognise that working virtually will involve working differently.

In particular, basic communications skills such as listening, focusing and engaging with others are required at a level that may not be expected or possessed, but need to be developed to a high level.

Furthermore, s/he needs to be aware that the hygiene factors of privacy and timing are critical. I also cover the implications of amplification of feelings and reactions, especially with respect to silences in the virtual space.

One of the overriding themes emerging from the interviews with the MilkCo leaders was the realisation that, by working and leading in the context of MilkCo's virtual strategy process, they discovered what some of them called 'a new discipline'. They explained to me that they had been working virtually for several years, using teleconferences, video-conferences (which they soon identified as not very helpful) and so-called net-meetings (web-based virtual meetings), but they felt that this was completely different from what they did in the context of the virtual strategy process.

Whereas before they were only exchanging information and monitoring the progress of some projects, they now realised that it was possible actually to think together, co-create new concepts and do 'real work', as some put it. However, the biggest realisation was that this was a new discipline, in the sense that they had to learn to work and connect differently with their colleagues in the virtual space. Here is a sample of quotes from my interviews:

- *"It was new territory for us. It is a new field and a new feeling that we needed to go into. You can't run it [these meetings] in the way that you have done before. It is a new area of competence even".*

- *"We understood that we have to do things differently, that there was something that we needed to learn".*

- *"The question of getting people on board with this virtual way of*

*working is critical. Everybody has to be trained, and needs to under-
stand what it is [...]. People need to understand that it is not a
'normal' teleconference".*

- *"There are new behaviours that you have to learn. You have to push
  yourself to be more pro-active, to take an initiative. In face-to-face
  interaction you can get away with having a lower level of concentration. Virtually you have to ask people more 'what do you mean?';
  otherwise you might isolate yourself".*

- *"I began to see the virtual meetings as a discipline per se. Before, I
  didn't look at it as something you need to learn to master, as a new
  discipline [...] I looked at it more as a technology than as competences.
  [...] It was very rewarding. An eye opening exercise. It was very fruitful.
  It was about discovering something new".*

Learning how to 'tune-in'

Several MilkCo managers as well as Sten underlined the need to 'tune into' a
new way of working and relating. One MilkCo person mentioned:

*"It is about getting everybody into the mode of working virtually. It is difficult
to switch off [from ongoing preoccupations] and you have to learn to tune-in".*

During our second session, I asked Sten to describe when he feels he is at
his best in a virtual environment. He answered without hesitation:

*"... when I call her [Sten is speaking about a member of his team] and I have
prepared an agenda for our exchange".*

Sten explained how much he struggled when she called him spontaneously and wanted to discuss things with him. He explained that he found it
difficult to 'get in the zone' and listen well when she asked him to do so
without scheduling their conversation beforehand. Sten claimed that for him
'it is a discipline in virtual leadership' to switch off and 'to have only a piece
of paper and shut the blinds in your office' to focus only on the person calling
you.

One device I have developed for the leaders I work with virtually is a
so-called 'focus exercise'. In the context of my research, several experiments
that I did with clients led me to realise the importance of being well aware of
one's body and bodily sensations when doing virtual work. The reason for
this is to avoid projecting one's own feelings and emotions on to others in the
virtual space, and/or the psychological phenomenon of 'confluence' where
one gets into a kind of symbiosis with somebody, making it impossible to
distinguish between the two worlds (my world and the world of the other).

In my experience, people tend to project their feelings and emotions more often and more easily in virtual meetings than in face-to-face ones, probably because of the lack of visual points of references related to the other people involved. This phenomenon might make healthy connections between people difficult and tricky. Hence, paradoxically, the more people are aware of their own body the better they are able to develop healthy relationships with others in the virtual space.

In order to help my clients to be as grounded as possible and enter into a 'healthy' connection with others in the virtual space, I developed the above mentioned **focus exercise**. The exercise consists of a guided journey through one's body to explore all bodily sensations. It lasts between eight and ten minutes and can be compared to meditational practice, where bodily aware-ness is the prime objective. (The focus exercise I use is described in more detail in Tool Box C.) As a practitioner, it is important for me to contract with my clients beforehand that we will do this exercise, and to help them understand why, in order to avoid any uneasy sense of esotericism, particu-larly for people not used to this kind of practice.

Most participants find the exercise a bit weird at the start, but the majority soon come to the conclusion that it is a healthy discipline to work well virtu-ally. The following words from one participant illustrate pretty well what participants feel and think about the exercise:

> "The first time I thought ... oh ... where are we going with that? Afterwards I realised that it was absolutely key".

Nevertheless, most leaders also say to me that they cannot imagine taking their team members through such an exercise, as this might be too big a leap for them. While it is acceptable for the team to do the exercise in a virtual team training or coaching situation, it is much more difficult for them to embed this discipline in their on-going practice. Virtual leaders often fear that they might be perceived as esoteric or crazy. I fully understand and respect this. However, I would still gently but surely challenge their anticipa-tion or fear and encourage them to experiment.

I also believe profoundly that they need to feel sufficiently confident with how they want to lead virtually. Again it is not about imposing on them **the** profile of the successful virtual leader but much more about encouraging them to experiment in the virtual space and become the virtual leader that they will become. I often offer to the sceptical ones the alternative of doing the exercise on their own before the virtual team meeting so that they can at least anchor themselves sufficiently well in their own bodily awareness and contain the virtual meeting in a robust way.

Learning to work with silences

One key challenge I have observed over time is the need for people to learn to work with silences in the virtual space. People actually communicate not only when they speak but also when they do not speak. Silences represent integrative parts of conversations, also in face-to-face situations. However we tend to notice silences less in the face-to-face, as we are more distracted by visual stimuli linked to the surroundings and our conversation partners.

The virtual space tends to amplify everything, given the less rich multi-sensorial environment. Hence a silence of one minute in face-to-face might feel like a silence of three minutes in the virtual space. Most people tend to feel uncomfortable with silences, and tend to fill silent moments during a teleconference or a web-based conference. They either repeat things they said before or provide more (often unnecessary) information just to break the silence that they find uncomfortable. At times they even ask people directly why they are silent or what they are thinking.

This might be fine in some instances, however people on the receiving end often feel 'put on the spot' and obliged to say something and make a point at a time when they might not be able to. This often leads to unhelpful patterns of communication where all feel that they need to state a point of view to be 'seen' in the virtual space and leaves little chance for a real dialogue to take place. Besides, this takes little account of the need some individuals have to think first on their own before they speak. Why should these people run the risk of being perceived as 'absent' virtually, although they might actually be doing some heavy thinking work before asking the key question or making the pivotal statement or suggestion?

Furthermore, although the topic of silences has not been explored much in our Western civilisations, the meaning of silence can be substantial in some Asian cultures. For example Japanese use silence to preserve harmony and East Asian participants are likely to regard silence as desirable and respectful when communicating with superiors in the virtual space (Panteli & Fineman 2006). My experience of working with many Asian people certainly has taught me the importance of respecting the silence and learning how to explore it without making people feel offended or under pressure.

Working effectively with silences means:

- Slowing down and resisting the drive to get on with the agenda

- Normalising the silence (by looking at it as an integrative part of the conversation and not as something to be avoided) for oneself and the team

- Exploring the silence in a way that invites people to share what is going on for them just in that one moment. A way to do that might be: 'I am noticing the silence and want to let it unfold for a while.' Or 'I am noticing the silence and wonder what it is telling us about the team' instead of asking: 'Peter, what do you think?'

- Bear in mind that silences are often pregnant with lots of meaning – trusting one's own intuition to make sense of it is a way to engage with others in the space.

- In summary working with silence means: **Don't fill the silence, feel it!**

Relearning the basics

One of my virtual coachees mentioned once that he felt that the leader in particular was more exposed in the virtual space than in a face-to-face meeting:

"You are in a very exposed situation, like in a goldfish bowl. The chairman is more under scrutiny than in the face-to-face".

He explained that people would listen more intensively in the virtual space and see more quickly and more clearly the possible disconnections between arguments. He also explained that the style of the leader (as well as of the other team members) would be exposed more quickly in its positive aspects, but also in its downsides. This meant for him that he would be more focused on how he felt, what he wanted to say and how he would say it.

Personally I find the analogy of the goldfish bowl very relevant, again for the simple reason that everything gets amplified in the virtual space. Personal traits and behaviours are more visible virtually than they might be face-to-face. The person in question needs to be aware of this and work with this awareness. For example in the context of my coaching role, I gave feedback to one member of the team that when he got excited about something (either positively or negatively) his way of speaking would become very fast and his voice very loud and hard, to the point where it might become difficult for others to understand him.

He responded that he had not realised this, but that this was also happening in face-to-face encounters. As a result of our conversation he paid a lot of attention to his emotions and, with this increased awareness, chose different ways of expressing his excitement in the virtual space, either by being more explicit about it with the team or by making a conscious decision to keep this awareness to himself for a while and decide in his own time what he needed to do as a result. Another interviewee mentioned how he realised quickly that he had no choice but to work differently with his emotions because these became much more noticeable in the virtual space:

"You become much more aware of your own reactions. After the first meeting I realised that I became very irritated by two people in particular. Whereas in the face-to-face I would have acted on this immediately, in these circumstances I stayed with this irritation and started thinking: Is this about me? I started reflecting more".

The examples above underline the need that virtual leaders might feel in becoming much more aware of some key aspects of human interaction, such as presence, listening carefully, dealing with your own emotions and reflecting intensively about yourself in the space.

These aspects are nothing new per se, in fact one interviewee mentioned:

"I have learnt things that I now apply in the face-to-face. It is about becoming aware again. What I have learnt in particular from this virtual process is that I need to involve others more, also in the face-to-face. It is all about presence. It is not because they are physically present that they are present!"

As a result this interviewee explained to me that he learnt to go slower in the virtual space, to pay more attention to the relationships around the virtual table and to the level of presence in the space:

"In virtual meetings it is mandatory to do this. I also now slow down in face-to-face meetings as I have realised that I will save time in the end".

Indeed if these aspects are nothing new, they require nevertheless a new mode of working and a mental shift to give them the importance that they deserve. Key aspects of this 'new mode' include the need to be focused specifically on oneself and others in the virtual space, as well as the willingness to deal with the amplified patterns that might be brought to light in the virtual space.

Sten and William had the same learning (see Appendix for description of my co-researchers). On the day I had my final conversation with Sten I asked him what he felt he had learnt from his virtual leadership experiments. He answered quickly:

"I don't like the way I run my face-to-face meetings any longer. We actually don't connect with each other. We don't listen. We are not present to each other".

William had a very similar reaction in one of our sessions:

"I don't like our face-to-face meetings where I sit at the top of the table and we have our endless PowerPoint presentations. I want to be more engaged with my people. I want us to be better connected with each other. I have decided to stop all PowerPoint, or at least to have only one or two slides with key figures".

I remember another story relating to this theme. I was invited to talk in London about virtual leadership in front of 30 managers (what I would call a typical mix of the very sceptical, the curious, those experienced in virtual working but frustrated, and the experienced but still curious people). I had invited one of my clients, Rainer from InterCo with whom, and with whose team, I had done a lot of work on virtual leadership. During the presentation we talked about the importance of listening in the virtual space. I still remember Rainer's deep concentration and efforts to describe what listening means for him in the virtual space, and in contrast some bored faces of attendees, with their eyes rolled upwards, thinking so strongly that I could almost hear them:

"Here we go again. Listening. This is truly nothing new".

After the presentation Rainer was still very excited and his face was slightly red with frustration, almost anger:

"They all say that they know what good listening means and that they are good listeners. They have no clue! They first need to learn to do this virtually then they will know!"

This story, which I have experienced repeatedly with many variations, shows that people usually expect ground-breaking new ways of leading virtually, but the most important thing is actually about revisiting the basics to develop new awareness.

Unlearning bad habits

Another big challenge for leaders in the virtual space is to realise that some habits developed throughout the years of virtual working are actually pretty damaging for the development of good virtual connectivity. It often takes me a lot of time and effort to explain to participants why these habits are actually 'bad habits' which are getting in their way; however as soon as they experience how different a virtual meeting can be when applying new principles, they usually adopt these with no further discussion.

I would like to illustrate the main 'bad habits', which can be serious hurdles to effective virtual leadership and high performance in the virtual space.

Virtual meetings, precisely because they take place in the virtual space, need to be organised and led in a way that takes into account the idiosyncrasies of the medium, with all the consequences that these might have in terms of team dynamics and psychology.

Very often however virtual meetings, either in the form of teleconferences or web-meetings, do not receive the status and attention that they deserve and are squeezed in between face-to-face meetings or held (at least the tele-conferences) in the car, the airport lounge, the train, or any other public place. This leads to several unfortunate consequences, with significant impact on the virtual experience, and hence the results achieved in the space. Here are a few examples to illustrate this point.

When people call in from a public place they underestimate that background noise, which is significantly amplified in the virtual space, becomes a strong disruption for all attendees. This not only gets in the way of good comprehension but tends, very understandably, to irritate the participants who have made the effort to be alone and undisturbed in a quiet place. Unfortunately this behaviour rarely gets challenged and discussed. People tolerate it and do not show their annoyance; this in turn gets in the way of good relationship building.

Another parameter that deserves particular attention in the virtual space is the process used to decide on the start and end times of meetings when all meet synchronously.* I observe that companies tend to set timings according to the Headquarters' time zone, and to forget that this might mean getting up at 3.00 am for some people or working until midnight for others. Admittedly these timing difficulties may be unavoidable if one leads a team spread across the globe, but the problem is exacerbated when people do not agree on the timing in a transparent way.

Considering perhaps alternating who will have to get up in the middle of the night on different occasions can have a very positive effect. In other words, scheduling virtual meetings as opposed to face-to-face ones is not a simple process of identifying a date, but involves careful consideration and conversations requiring sensibility and sensitivity. In Tool Box D you will find a simple practical tool to engage your team in a productive decision-making process to fix timings for virtual meetings in a way that feels acceptable and respectful for all involved.

When people agree to meet virtually, those based in the same building (again often the Headquarters group) tend to gather in the same room while others are linked in via a phone line. Many of us have experienced lengthy teleconferences spent around a speaker phone, then, having spoken potentially controversial words has had a strange feeling of being anxious about the subsequent silence on the line. For the one who is alone on a phone link the silence can feel very long. That person will probably think: 'Why is nobody responding? Do they think my argument is stupid? What are the

---

*   Synchronous mode: people in different places connect at the same time (independently of their time zones), for example in a phone conference or a web conference, as opposed to – Asynchronous mode: people in different places connect with each other at different points of time (for example in a blog). See glossary for a more detailed explanation.

others saying to each other in the room? What faces are they making about me?'

This example illustrates another mistake in virtual working – allowing a mix of solitary and group participation – that will automatically count against trust-building. Hence I recommend to team leaders that, particularly if they are to work on complex issues with their team, they need to ask everybody to be linked in virtually. This may require courage, as some team members might think: 'What's all the fuss about? Why can't we just sit together as we're in the same building anyway?' The leader needs the courage to challenge ingrained habits, and the ability to explain why the mix of face-to-face and virtual settings can lead to difficult team dynamics in the virtual space.

Admittedly, challenging ingrained habits might not be sufficient in this instance. In some cases this might also mean challenging the office design. What was once considered as the solution for improved communication, namely the open plan office, suddenly becomes a real barrier to effective communication in the virtual space. Given their office layout, some organisations find it difficult if not impossible to provide sufficient personal space in the form of closed offices from where employees can work virtually. In some cases working from home will also represent a challenge due to either national or company regulations. In other cases working from home is a sheer impossibility because employees have houses that are too small to find the necessary personal space to isolate themselves and work virtually.

These difficulties exist and need to be addressed. Leaders and HR professionals may need to be petitioned here. The solution does not have to be complicated. For example one of my clients, keen to put an end to the disruptive 'bad habits', installed so-called 'cockpits' in their offices, where people can find the necessary – albeit small – personal physical space to concentrate and connect well in the virtual space.

For some readers the examples mentioned might feel like details, and they might be wondering why I am spending time mentioning and explaining them. Several years of practice and research have taught me that these small matters do make a big difference when it comes to the quality of engagement and the dynamics in the team, which in turn impacts directly on the team performance. Implementing these aspects alongside many others that are still to be mentioned requires that the person in charge of the team not only has the courage to challenge entrenched team behaviours, but also models these new ways of meeting virtually. *Leadership is asked for: management does not suffice!*

So what?

If you are truly prepared to practice the discipline of virtual leadership then:

Learn

- How to tune-in into the virtual space to connect effectively with others and to avoid collusion

- How to work with silences and realise that silent people are not necessarily absent

- How to become more aware of emotions and make conscious choices about how to use them

Relearn

- The basics of listening

- The basics of engaging with people into productive conversations (see Tool Box F)

Unlearn

- The bad habits that you might have developed over time virtually and create your own 'virtual' working hygiene. For example insist that everybody is connected virtually (no mix of face-to-face and virtual connections) and that everybody is alone, undisturbed and in a quiet space. See Tool Box A: Summary of hygiene principles for virtual synchronous meetings.

INVITATION 2
Listen, Forget Body Language!

With this invitation I make the point that, through our virtual work in audio and web-and-audio based environments, we can develop a different listening ability, a sharper sense of connectedness with others in the field, a kind of seventh sense that enables us to connect at a deeper level (than in face-to-face) with ourselves, others and the universe. Most management and leadership training has been closely focused on the visual and has privileged body language. To be effective in the virtual space leaders will need to develop the capacity to listen differently and more deeply.

One hypothesis I hold as to why working virtually in the synchronous (see glossary) space invites people to become more aware of themselves and others in terms of how they behave, feel, and relate to each other is precisely the lack of body language (assuming that people use a web-based platform where everybody can work on documents together and are connected by the phone but not by cameras). I have developed this hypothesis over seven years of practising virtual/audio action learning based on the feedback that I have received regularly from the participants in my virtual sets.

Paradoxically, when they work in a virtual action learning environment people feel that their sense-making of themselves and the others in the space slows down, but they get faster at identifying what really matters for the person sharing an issue, and they connect at a deeper level (than in face-to-face). (Caulat 2004)

When I facilitated the critically-important internal workshop with my Doctoral peers some had a strong reaction to the fact that they could not see each other. Sibel explained:

"What struck me yesterday [...] I was missing faces. I had no sense of people. I had no faces of people to look at".

At this point Alison explained that she uses photographs when she does coaching on the phone.

Ronald also had a strong reaction to the missing faces and introduced the concept of the 'group imago':

> *"Unless one person is speaking, I don't get a sense of anyone else being here, except when I get a message [through the chat room] ... but I don't have a sense of us as a collective. I have a sense of someone when they speak. I don't have a sense of them when they don't speak".*

So while Sibel and possibly Alison needed to see others to develop some sense of their presence, Ronald at a minimum needed an ongoing vocal contact to develop the sense of the presence of others.

Cindy, on the other hand, seemed to be well-connected and with a good sense of our peers in the group through her activities with others on the whiteboard while we were speaking with each other (on WebEx, participants can open an empty slide – a 'whiteboard' – and draw or write on it together). So it seemed did Isabelle, who explained how much she enjoyed the 'shared doodling', giving her a sense of connectedness and helping her to focus. When I listened to the recording I noticed indeed what I would call a good moment of connectedness and intimacy.

Mark also felt very connected and had a strong sense of togetherness. He explained:

> *"I did have a very strong sense of community. I felt people with and around me [...]. It was a different sense of a group for me. In the face-to-face setting I find the circle constraining. I didn't feel confined on that day. It was a liberating sense of the group/community".*

He carried on explaining:

> *"The day for me was quite memorable. I still have vivid images of the day [...]. The conversation with Sophie was very intense [Mark is referring here to the moment when my peers were transferred into virtual breakout rooms to discuss in pairs their experiences so far of working virtually] [...], when you came to tell us to come back to the main room I had an image of you coming into my room to tell me 'Now it is time'".*

I find the diversity of experiences in terms of connectedness quite striking, and I wonder what it would take for a leader working virtually to deal with the variety of needs and responses.

I also believe that the awareness of one's own response is a critical starting point. When I work with clients with no camera and one participant expresses how much s/he misses seeing the faces of others, I gently but firmly invite him/her not to work from a deficit based perspective (by looking at what one is missing compared with the face-to-face) but to focus on what one has. So far I have felt encouraged to carry on doing so, because my experience has been that after a while participants get used to not seeing each other's faces, and start explaining how much more intensively they listen to what is said.

Generally my own experience, based on several video conferences I did a few years ago, has been that, when working remotely, watching the faces of people can quickly become more of a distraction than an enabler especially when the technology is not first rate. This hypothesis is often confirmed when I ask clients for their point of view. The dominant opinion is that they prefer to use audio and Internet-based technologies with no video facilities, because the video does not bring clear benefits and does not always justify the additional effort and cost. As a further example, Williams, an experienced virtual facilitator and coach, writes:

> "In fact sometimes we can miss the essence of a person's message while trying to read body language. Body language can sometimes take away from listening" (2002, p.20).

Video will always be only a substitute for face-to-face

I am still intrigued though by the fact that most people, when they start working virtually, initially strongly want to have the visual comfort of seeing each other. I assume that this has to do with our attachment to what we know best. I also notice that diverse technology companies are working very hard to develop more flexible, better quality, video facilities for virtual working. Yet it is still unclear to me how a group of 40 people can get connected virtually and see each other at the same time. Technology might get there at some point.

Actually Telepresence from Cisco and/or the Tandberg technology seem to be on the way and currently are gaining a growing share of the market for virtual communication media. Nevertheless, people using this medium explained to me that they are still struggling to get eye contact with other attendees, because people tend to look at the camera instead of looking at the attendees via a video link.

Furthermore this technology is still very expensive: in some of my clients' organisations the rooms equipped with Telepresence need to be booked months in advance, which is perceived by the users as somehow contradictory to the just-in-time modus operandi that other virtual communication technologies offer. These could be seen as secondary hurdles which I assume might be overcome with time when technology has progressed. But my personal belief is that a strong sense of virtual connectivity can be developed specifically without seeing each other's faces. Using the visual channel might actually lock people into a substitute modus operandi (for the face-to-face) whereas non-visual channels offer new and different ways of connecting with each other and, if used well, can open up a new path with a potentially more powerful way to connect.

I had not been particularly vocal about this for a while as I feared that people might think that I was biased towards some technologies as opposed to others. To my surprise though, at a meeting with several clients where we were discussing the topic of virtual leadership, one of the attendees, working for a leading global telecommunication company, stated:

> *"But the use of cameras and Telepresence is only a substitute for the face-to-face and actually takes away the potential for higher connectivity that exists in the virtual environment".*

I could not agree more: while video-conferences will always remain only a substitute for face-to-face, audio and web-based virtual environments offer a real chance to break through the face-to-face paradigm and connect with others and the universe in an even more powerful way.

Actually I find some justification for this view in several disciplines that I would now like to explore.

The voice is pregnant with whom we are

Perls (1969), the founder of the Gestalt school of psychology, explains how key the voice is as an expression of the essence of a person. For Heron the voice 'is pregnant with whom you really are' (1999, p.234). Gilligan et al (2006), who developed the so-called Listening Guide as a method of psychological analysis, also underlines clearly the importance of the voice:

> *"Thus, each person's voice is distinct – a footprint of the psyche, bearing the marks of the body, of that person's history, of culture in the form of language, and the myriad ways in which human society and history shape the voice and thus leave their imprints on the human soul".* (Idem 2006, pp.253-254)

She then demonstrates that listening to the voice of a person is a crucial way to enter truly into a relationship with that person.

When I started working virtually I realised how much I still needed to train my listening in order to hear the several components of the voice (pitch, tone, rhythm, etc.) and I actually taught myself to listen more carefully beyond the words. I now often have the experience that, for example, when a friend calls me I quickly notice whether s/he is well or tired, nervous, or sick before even asking how s/he is doing. I have tested my understanding several times by saying what I heard (or what I was reading in the voice) and a few times I have had the reaction: "How do you know?" I hear more and more stories of other people who do the same thing with similar experiences and outcomes. So my growing hypothesis is that listening is a way to connect intensively with somebody, not only at the intellectual level but at the emotional level, particularly in the virtual environment where there are no visual distractions.

Multi-layered listening is like a muscle that everybody can learn to flex more and more. When I run a virtual leadership workshop one of the exercises I do is the 'three levels of listening' exercise. This is an Ashridge exercise that we also use in face-to-face meetings, where we invite participants to listen in to three different channels: the content of what is being said, the emotions and feelings the speaker is going through, and the intuition of the listener – what their gut is telling them about what they are hearing. Participants in the virtual leadership workshops usually enjoy the exercise because they find it very enabling. They often say that it helps them to 'see' in the virtual environment. Recently one of the participants of InterCo told me that the biggest learning for him was to listen differently when he is on the phone with others.

Slower is faster

Isaacs (1999) emphasises the central role of hearing and listening. He shows how in Western cultures we tend to privilege seeing because our culture is dominated by sight:

> "The result of this external bombardment of visual impressions is that we tend to think in these ways. In the Western world we have begun to be habituated to this quick pace, and are impatient with other rhythms. But seeing and listening are very different. The substance of seeing is light. Light moves at a far more rapid pace than sound: 186,000 miles per second as opposed to 1,100 feet per second. (Metric: light is almost 300,000,000 mps, whereas sound is only 330 mps.) In other words, to listen you must slow down (sic) and operate at the speed of sound rather than at the speed of light. The eye seems to perceive at a superficial level, at the level of reflected light.* While the eye sees at the surface, the ear tends to penetrate below the surface". (1999, p.86)

In his book *"Nada Brahma. Die Welt ist Klang"* (2007) ("Nada Brahma: The world is sound") the famous German jazz author Berendt points out that the ear is the only sense that fuses an ability to measure with an ability to judge. This means that while there are many optical illusions, Berendt explains that there are few acoustic illusions: "the ears do not lie". He carries

---

* Footnote from the author: This was one of the reasons Plato mistrusted the 'mimetic', or image based, artists; his fear was that they would distort people's sense of reality.

on by explaining how he noticed that in our Western world we have a seeing hypertrophy and cannot hear properly any longer. For him 'seeing' can remain at the surface while hearing automatically goes in-depth:

> *"The eye touches the surface. But nothing can be perceived by the ear without penetrating. Even when something is only loosely heard, it will go deeper than the look. The 'hearing' person has therefore more chances to go in-depth than the 'seeing' one".* (Idem, pp.19–20 – translated from German text)

Berendt continues that if we want an in-depth change of our conscience (which he argues is necessary in our current world) we need to counterbalance the 'seeing' hypertrophy and develop our 'hearing' equally well.

Isaacs agrees with Berendt and adds:

> *"The sense of hearing gives us a remarkable connection with the invisible, underlying order of things. Through our ears we gain access to vibration, which underlies everything around us. The sense of tone and music in another's voice gives us an enormous amount of information about that person, about their stance toward life, about their intentions".* (Isaacs 1999 p.86)

Based on my personal experience and my experience of working with clients, I fully agree with Isaacs. I also see a clear link with Foulkes' (1975) concept of 'matrix'. According to Foulkes a group is not just a collection of several individual 'unconsciousnesses', but has a common unconscious, revealing itself in the 'matrix'. Foulkes speaks of 'resonance' as if individuals in a group were connected to each other by a web of mental processes which join and pass through them. My hypothesis is that by slowing down and listening, particularly in a virtual space with no visual stimulation of embodied others, we connect at a deeper level than in face-to-face and activate the resonance between people. As mentioned, I have experienced this several times in the context of my practice of virtual action learning and have explored this at length in my Master's degree thesis dedicated to virtual action learning (Caulat 2004).

The myth of body language

The interesting thing is, however, that almost every time I share my view about the untapped potential of the auditory in the virtual space, the leaders I work with mention that this view goes against what has been transmitted over time about the power of body language, with the well-known adage that 78% of the meaning of somebody's statement comes through his/her body language and not through the words used. Having done some further research into this, I found that Mehrabian, whose research is at the origin of this belief, has been misunderstood and that his findings have been simplified to such a degree over time that they have become inaccurate.

In his studies, first published in 1971, Mehrabian came to two conclusions. Firstly, that there are basically three elements in any face-to-face communication: words, tone of voice and facial expression; and secondly that the non-verbal elements are particularly important for communicating *feelings* and *attitude*, especially when they are *incongruent*. In other words, if the words spoken are incongruous with the tone of voice and facial expression, people tend to believe the tonality and facial expression. According to Mehrabian (1971), these *three elements* account differently for our *liking* for the person who expresses his/her feelings: words account for 7%, tone of voice accounts for 38%, and body language accounts for 55% of the liking. They are often abbreviated as the "3 Vs" for Verbal, Vocal & Visual. On his webpage Mehrabian clearly states this:

> "(...) Total Liking = 7% Verbal Liking + 38% Vocal Liking + 55% Facial Liking: *Please note that this and other equations regarding relative importance of verbal and non-verbal messages were derived from experiments dealing with communications of feelings and attitudes (i.e, like-dislike). Unless a communicator is talking about their feelings or attitudes, these equations are not applicable"*.

The above does **not** mean that non-verbal elements convey the bulk of the message in all cases.

So where does this digression leave me regarding Sibel's, Alison's and Ronald's sense of missing the feeling of connectedness? Is there something about getting used to this virtual environment little by little and developing stronger listening skills, as I suggested previously? Is there also something about virtual working (at least audio and web based synchronous virtual working) feeling more natural to people having an auditory preference as opposed to those who have a visual or kinaesthetic preference (using the Neuro-Linguistic Programming model, Bandler and Grinder 1979). Although I know that I have a visual preference in NLP terms (I tend to engage better with ideas if I can picture them) I would not say that I have difficulties in connecting at a deeper level with others in a virtual space; however, as mentioned above, I have had to learn to do it.

Not seeing embodied others frees you up!

Not seeing people's faces undoubtedly presents some advantages at an even more practical level. Some people claim that they feel freer to think and work mentally when they do this in the virtual (non-video based) space. For example, as I was doing some experimentation with audio action learning

---

* Source: www.kaaj.com/psych/smorder/html – viewed on 27th March 2010

one manager of ComTel, Mina, a Finnish lady, said that at times she was getting really caught up in the conversation and kept jumping off the bed and walking around in the room:

"I was really involved physically in the conversation. If somebody had been watching me, they would have thought that I was mad".

She explained that in the session she felt freed up from all the conventions and rules that exist in the Finnish meeting culture, where people feel that they should have very limited body movement and facial expression:

"Finnish culture really restricts your behaviour in face-to-face; even your body movements to be honest, even your facial expressions become somehow really restricted".

She felt that she could do what she wanted without infringing the rules:

"Maybe that gives you the permission, the freedom to express your thoughts and feelings in a different way [when working virtually, with no camera]" (Caulat 2004, p.55).

Thinking of myself, whether I am facilitating or leading, in a virtual context I tend to be more daring, probing, sharper in my interventions with authority figures than when I work face-to-face with them. For example, I facilitated several virtual conferences with people from all over the world for RasCo. The attendees were key external stakeholders for the organisation in question and were for the most part well-known personalities in several disciplines. After one of these sessions, which turned out to be lively and engaging, I noted in my journal:

"My god I am almost shocked about how as a facilitator I dared to challenge Mr. R., ex-Minister in Brazil, and how straightforward I was with him".

The same happened when I was facilitating a virtual large group conference with 47 people, including the CEO of TamCo. I felt no anxiety about working with them, on the contrary I enjoyed questioning them, probing, testing, etc. For me the lack of visual clues proves to be an enabler rather than a disabler. It is as if I feel more equal to figures of authority in the virtual space. The theme and feeling of greater equality with figures of authority has been mentioned repeatedly with the leaders I work with in the virtual space.

So what?

- If you are used to video-conferences, experiment without a camera

- Accept the fact that you cannot see your colleagues in the virtual space as a real chance to learn to connect differently with them

- Learn to listen with your intuition

- Listen to feelings and emotions, not only to words

- Slow down - don't forget: slower is faster (see Tool Box G)

- Create the right environment for you and others to listen well

- Equip yourself with the right headset covering both ears and use good quality phone lines. (See Tool Box A for more practical guidance)

INVITATION 3
Don't Control, Connect!

This section illustrates how the virtual leader needs to be ready radically to reconsider his/her notions of 'being present', 'here and now' and to let go of the desire to control what others do in the virtual space. S/he needs to develop the skill to sense others' presence and to win their attention. It is about increasing 'share of ear' as opposed to 'share of voice': What counts is not how much you say but rather how much you attract people's attention by listening well to them.

I often experience the following patterns: when I officially start a workshop face-to-face and greet everybody in the circle, everything stops and paradoxically all lively conversations come to an end. This can be different in the virtual space: I might indeed officially start the day with a group, but informal conversations might go on among individuals, for example in the chat room of the virtual platform, or even via email or text messages. The virtual space allows the formal and informal to co-exist with the same weight. In some 'formal' moments of virtual working I am pretty sure that the informal exchange might actually be more active and vivid than ever. There is some kind of linearity, and hence separation, that exists in the face-to-face when it comes to the formal and the informal.

Usually in a meeting people have the informal conversations relating to formal talks, either after the meeting or in the break. How often have you led a difficult meeting, and decided to take a break to create a 'fresh start'? This works well on so many occasions! While progress after the break may simply be due to the participants having renewed energy, it is often the case that informal conversations have prompted the unblocking. The informal has thus been very helpful, even essential. I would argue that the challenge of bringing the informal into the formal still remains in the virtual space.

It is interesting to notice that most of the people I know, and who are used to working virtually in their organisation, have developed strict working etiquettes in the spirit of increasing the efficiency of the virtual exchange; yet this seems to make the formal even more stifled. For example, in most teleconference etiquettes people are asked to say their name before they speak, and interrupting somebody is seen as an absolute no-go. Even worse, on some of the internet-based platforms (for example Centra or Interwise, at least in their original versions) people need to ask for permission to talk; unless the chair of the virtual meeting activates their microphone for them, they are not able to make themselves heard, the purpose being to maintain a clear focus on the task and on the person chairing the meeting. One could argue that the focus of these platforms is on the task and the leader as opposed to the followers.

However, one can also weave the informal into the formal by allowing every participant to use all available means of communication on the platform, and to share what they are doing as they go along. Obviously, I don't know to what extent people would be willing to share all their informal and personal exchanges, and I assume that it would be neither possible, nor even desirable. I also think that it might require different skills, and perhaps more importantly a different mindset, on the facilitator's and/or leader's and participants' sides for it to happen in a natural and generative way. Personally I am clear that interweaving the formal and informal would require further acceptance of the informal as an integral part of a meeting. I admit that at times I still hear my inner voice telling me: 'They are having private chats, so they can't be listening properly to what we are doing; they are not concentrating hard enough!' From my conversations with virtual leaders I can claim that most of them think the same at times:

"How can I know whether they listen? Might they be doing their emails while attending the virtual meeting? Please give me a tool to stop this! How can I control them?"

My usual answer is: Don't even try! If there is something that cannot be achieved virtually, it is precisely the control of others.

Most virtual platforms allow you to decide whether the participants in a meeting can or cannot use the chat tools among themselves. A recent addition to the features on the WebEx platform enables the person leading or facilitating the meeting to see a small symbol letting him/her know whether the attendee is watching the same slide as the one s/he is showing. However, I encourage virtual leaders not to even try to control their team members' movements. My explanation to them is: 'As long as you sense that they are really engaged with you and with all team members, as long as you make progress in whatever you are doing, it does not really matter if they are having private chats or writing their emails. By having private informal exchanges they might be helping each other.' I often hear surprise if not shock on the other end of the line when I say this.

Multitasking can be good!

My Doctoral peer Mark's reflection about the first day of the virtual work-shop was:

> *"I would not run through four different conversations at the same time. This feels quite abnormal".*

Mark was referring to the fact that he was having several exchanges of emails with different people, as well as exchanges in the chat room, whilst also working with the group. I actually agree with Mark that it might feel quite abnormal, and at the same time I know that this is the case for most virtual interactions between people. This is actually what most virtual leaders complain about at the beginning. So what do 'normal' and 'abnormal' mean? From a facilitator's point of view, and maybe even more so from a virtual leader's point of view, the key question is: if Mark had four different conversations at the same time, does it mean that he was less engaged than he might have been in a face-to-face setting? Does it mean that the quality of his engagement was less good? I was burning to pose these questions to Mark. When I did so, he answered in the most amazing and helpful way.

I will now give you a bit more detail about what happened. Not yet knowing Mark's point of view, I wrote the following in my journal:

> *"I didn't feel that Mark was less engaged than when we sit in a face-to-face setting. He actually explained that he felt that the virtual setting was less oppressive than sitting in face-to-face circles. I wouldn't say that I felt that he was more engaged either, but his intervention in the virtual space felt very impactful to me. I could feel – for example when he shared his sense that organisational boundaries were coming down in the virtual space – how vivid his reflection had been".*

When I discussed this point with him later, he assured me that he was fully engaged with what was happening and he gave me a wonderful analogy to explain the nature of his engagement:

> *"For me, being in this virtual workshop was like flying in an aeroplane. When I fly with four to five other planes there are people on the intercom navigating me, then there is the radio control person, then I have internal chats on the private radio with other pilots. [...] I have all these ways of engaging when I fly an aeroplane, it's like on WebEx [...]. When we get back on the ground, what do we think really happened? Which conversations really happened? – all of them at the same time, with no one more important than another. It was the same for me on the day of the virtual workshop: what do we think really happened? [...] In the face-to-face the facilitator [or the chairman of a meeting] tends to hold the space. He can't do that on WebEx".*

In my view these words of Mark's describe beautifully how a leader and/or facilitator cannot control other people's activities in the virtual space or dictate their degree of engagement throughout.

> This finding is confirmed by research undertaken by Wasson (2004) who observed the members of five teams working virtually over a period of time. She comes to the conclusion that multi-tasking is something positive, as long as people are well trained and aware of when multi-tasking might be helpful and when not:
>
> *"Since long before the days of virtual meetings, employees have complained about face-to-face meetings as a poor use of their time. Many meetings were designed in ways that did not absorb the full attention of participants, leaving them feeling bored and frustrated. With the advent of virtual meetings, many employees feel relieved to be able to make more complete use of their attention resources"* (Wasson 2004).

In addition I would like to quote Suler (a) who offers a different concept of presence in the virtual space:

"Relationships in cyberspace encourage us to re-examine many of the traditional assumptions about presence implied in the Be Here Now maxim. As we have seen, the very notion of 'here' is called into question [...]. With practice, we learn how to manage a multi-tasking of presence. We can be here and now in one particular online system of environmental and interpersonal presences, while keeping an eye and ear open for something that might call our attention to another system – either the in-person setting or another online setting. Usually it is a change in one of the other environments that signals us to attend to it. [...] The process resembles mindfulness meditation in which we focus our presence on and with one thing, but also allow another part of our mind to silently notice and then shift concentration to other things that might arise from the wide range of possible presences in the periphery of our field of awareness. Rather than being one-dimensional, presence involves shifts in magnitude, direction, and juxtaposition as we balance and redirect our awareness from here to there".

I agree completely with Suler's view and find the provocation more than appropriate. I am tempted to challenge our views of presence in the face-to-face too: it is not because people look at you quietly and in a seemingly interested way that they actually do listen to you. In that specific moment they might actually be thinking of something totally different.

In this context Nevis's allusion (Nevis 2001) to Lewin is very helpful:

> "*A thorough phenomenologist, Lewin also saw that people in the same situation exist in different life-spaces. For instance, people who attend the same meeting are actually in varying psychological worlds. Whether they are attending to different sensory and mental stimuli or having different need tension systems, they will define their internal experience and their experience of the social and physical environment in unique ways*". (Nevis 2001, p.12)

So I would argue that the same patterns happen in the face-to-face space, but that in the virtual environment they are clearer, more obvious and people can work differently with them. This is precisely what one of the MilkCo leaders meant by:

> "*What I have learnt in particular from this virtual process is that I need to involve others more, both in the virtual and the face-to-face. It is all about presence*".

As mentioned in Invitation 1, it is not because people are physically present that they are present! In other words the virtual leader can achieve much more by asking open questions, slowing down and actually listening, rather than going into 'sending mode'.

Finally I would like to add a story from my work with the 'Digital Natives'. Maya and Elien explain to me how much they enjoy watching a film together while being physically apart, by using SMS. Both of them would watch a film, each in their respective home but would stay in contact throughout the film and would comment on it and exchange their views using SMS: 'It is nice to be able to discuss with a friend when watching a movie together'. I can't refrain from asking them how they manage at the same time to watch a film and SMS each other ('I would be afraid of missing something important in the film!' I say). Maya answers that it is often not 'an important movie' and that they don't really know why, but that it is fun to remain connected. It seems to me that in that instance not the film but more the SMS conversation is important and that the film provides them with a platform for them to converse and stay connected. Having explored this a bit further with them I realise how much I am stuck within my own patterns (where for example the film would have been the primary focus for me) and how much I am comparing in my head what could have been a face-to-face conversation with their ongoing SMS conversation.

Maya's spontaneous reaction suddenly makes me aware of that:

"You know, actually, that's a different conversation [one of another kind]. It's just fun to be connected this way!"

Actually, one could agree that this anecdote is much more than about the fun that Digital Natives have in the kind of situation related above. According to Prensky (2001,b) Digital Natives accustomed to multi-tasking and speedy activities crave interactivity and get quickly bored in environments where they are told things and asked to learn in a linear fashion. For them parallel thinking and random-access of information are the norm. Prensky explains that the latest research in neurobiology shows that stimulation of various kinds actually changes brain structures and affects the way people think. This is true for Digital Natives and might also be true for anybody else as the brain gets constantly reorganised in our child and adult lives. It is a phenomenon technically known as 'neuro-plasticity'. Prensky explains that children raised with the computer think differently from others, because their minds leap around and their cognitive structures become parallel and not sequential. He strongly disagrees with the statement that Digital Natives have shorter attention spans. According to him, Digital Natives can demonstrate long attention spans provided that interactivity and immediate response to their actions are given:

"So it generally isn't that Digital Natives can't (sic) pay attention, it's that they choose not to". (Prensky 2001,b)

Those among my readers who already lead 'Digital Natives' will be used to this type of completely natural behaviour and mind-set. Those who are not yet leading people like Maya and Elien had better get ready now!

Do take the time to connect at a personal level
Rather than spending time and effort trying to control what others do in the virtual space, I suggest that leaders spend time and effort connecting well at a personal level during a virtual meeting and inviting all members to do the same. A principle that I practise systematically and invite others to apply as well is at a start of a virtual (synchronous – see glossary) meeting to create the space for everybody to connect at a personal level, for example asking questions such as: how I am feeling right now; what is getting / might be getting in the way of my engagement in this space and what help I might

need to overcome this; what happened since last time we met; anything in particular I want you all to know; etc.

Dedicating the time and space for everybody to speak to these (or similar) questions will help people to connect at a deeper, more personal level before moving on to the task. More importantly it will make it easy and normal for people to admit that they are in a different space mentally speaking (not just physically speaking) – which is potentially difficult – and this will help the leader or facilitator, as well as everybody else in the team, to support the person in question in his/her efforts to connect.

In the same way as establishing this connection at the start of the meeting, closing the personal connection at the end is helpful in enabling people to move on, particularly when meetings have been intense. Closure needs to be achieved at an emotional and personal level as well as at a technical one. In the same way as people shake hands (or hug each other) at the end of a face-to-face meeting, people need a closing ritual virtually so that they can complete well with each other.

Unfortunately, I observe that the vast majority of leaders and/or teams working virtually do not have any connecting and disconnecting rituals. They dive directly into the task and might end up finishing later than scheduled, with people disappearing quietly from the meeting without others even noticing that they are not there any longer. In my view these practices (even if generated for good reasons such as not wanting to disrupt the meeting when leaving) are very counter-productive in terms of relationship and trust building.

When I discuss the importance of connecting and disconnecting rituals with virtual teams I often get challenged:

"But you cannot spend half hour connecting in a meeting of two hours!"

Actually, my experience has taught me that this connecting time is very well invested, time that will pay enormous dividends not only in the long term in relation to trust building but also in the short term for the reasons mentioned above.

So what?

The implications of the examples above might be perceived as counter-intuitive.

In order to succeed in the virtual space, when they chair meetings virtually, leaders can experiment with the following assumptions and suggestions:

- People *can* be in different places at the same time and actually be present

- Multitasking in the virtual space does not have to be something 'bad', on the contrary

- Incorporating the informal into the formal can be very positive

- Give up any need to control what people do

- Instead of exhibiting your need for control by saying a lot and control-ling the space through the technology and introducing limiting etiquettes, do listen carefully and develop a sense of people's engagement – you might also want to read Invitation 6 about power and control through technology and Tool Box F for ideas on engaging your team members' initial attention

- Do develop and practice your own connecting (and disconnecting) rituals so that people are strongly connected at a personal level before jumping to the task

- Finally, do not forget: If people feel listened to, they will truly attend and engage

INVITATION 4
Relationships Are All You Have!

The virtual leader needs to recognise relationships as **the** key pillar of his/her virtual leadership, and needs to be prepared to face challenges and a lack of understanding from traditional managers.
Building and nurturing relationships in the virtual space, and finding appropriate ways to do so, is an essential aspect of virtual leadership.

One of the key outcomes of my research is that it reinforces the fundamental importance of relationships when it comes to leading virtually. Rather than making my point and augmenting it with my co-researchers' views, I prefer to give an account of how one of my research groups (Silvia, Barbara and Matthew – see Appendix for further details) identified the importance of this aspect.

During our second session (at the first session we had agreed that each of us would share our reflections and experimentation) Barbara, CEO of an NGO very active in India and Africa in particular, took her turn and explained that she felt that most of her virtual leadership is based on the informal relationships that she develops with her counterparts in other countries. She suggested that this might be different for Matthew and Silvia, assuming that in 'corporate land', as she put it, there are lots of systems and processes on which to base one's virtual leadership. Matthew reacted by saying that Barbara seemed to think that 'the informal' is a bad thing. Silvia then also jumped in, saying:

> "All I have are the relationships. There are no real formal structures in the international key account management team, no monthly reports".

We then reflected on how everything might collapse for Silvia if she did not pay attention to building these relationships, as they are precisely the foundation for her virtual work.

Matthew added that, although there are plenty of structures and systems in place in his company

"You wouldn't be able to operate without the relationships".

We reflected on what this might mean, and used the machine metaphor to describe organisations. It seemed that in the traditional face-to-face working paradigm, relationships develop more in the informal anyway, and act as the essential 'oil' to make systems and processes work. This 'oil' might be indispensable, but it is not visible, and everybody focuses more on systems and processes. As it is not possible to meet somebody in the corridors of cyberspace by coincidence, the machine (the systems and processes) breaks down. Relationships and their importance become suddenly more 'visible', more tangible. Moving into the virtual space, the 'informal' within the traditional paradigm suddenly needs to become formalised, in the sense that one needs to make sure that it happens. Systems and processes cannot support virtual leaders unless they are combined with **active** relationships and these need to develop in an **active** way and cannot be left to coincidence.

We ended up agreeing that it is an essential role of the virtual leader to work on building these relationships, by bringing the informal into the formal virtual space. At this stage of our reflection Barbara interjected forcefully, underlining the core of our common view and sharing her frustration at the same time:

"The problem is the amount of time that I need to invest in building these relationships. What happens virtually doesn't get recognised. These relationships are so fragile – and nobody understands that in my organisation!"

Silvia immediately agreed vehemently with Barbara, explaining that she lives the same experience on a day-to-day basis:

"My struggle is to explain to my management how much time it takes to build these relationships. They keep telling me: 'You need to be more efficient'. They don't understand it!"

In our last session together, her frustration about this aspect was still vivid:

"It seems that I don't even reach them [her managers – who have no experience of leading virtually] with my efforts to explain the real importance of relationships [in the virtual space]".

At this stage the four of us agreed: we felt that there is a big gap in understanding, due largely to the fact that so few people really lead virtually. In particular Silvia and Barbara felt quite isolated, and not recognised in their efforts as relationship builders. Matthew agreed with that and spoke of a 'lack of shared experience'. Silvia spoke of 'ignorance'.

Virtual relationships are fragile but can be re-built fast

Silvia's words were very sharp and her intonation was strong. Her tone was full of anger. From my work with her on a one-to-one basis I can understand her feelings. Silvia had a bitter learning experience. We had spent several sessions exploring why and how she could develop more robust relationships, in particular with the Chinese members of her team. We had given substantial consideration to what an acceptable, yet personal, relationship in the virtual space with her Chinese colleagues could look like. Silvia had identified which of the themes she could discuss with each of her Chinese colleagues, and what personal information she could share with them. She was feeling positive about the progress that she had made with each member, the level of intimacy in the team and its performance.

Unfortunately, later in the year, Silvia was confronted with a variety of tough challenges, which she managed to cope with, but at the expense of the relationships that she had developed with the Chinese team. Our session at this point was bleak: Silvia was exhausted and disappointed. She felt that she had lost the connection with the Chinese team, and the business was not going well there. I felt her frustration, exhaustion and powerlessness at the disintegration of the team. I asked her for how long she had been unable to connect with them as she used to do (by teleconference, email and personal telephone calls). Silvia explained that she let everything slip approximately one month ago. We reflected together how amazed we both were at how quickly these relationships can break down, how fragile they are.

During the rest of the call I coached her to help her identify clearly for herself what was most important for her right now, given the immense amount of work and pressure on her shoulders. I was quietly surprised when she put work on rebuilding the relationships in first place. (At the beginning of our relationship just one year earlier, she had been most focused on getting the newest piece of information as a way to establish her legitimacy within her virtual team).

We then explored what she would like to do as a result. She was very clear that it was all about going back to the discipline of the relationship work that she had done before: teleconferences, phone calls, sharing more information by email, etc. At the end of the conversation I sensed that she was more positive and I felt some of her energy returning. She actually confirmed this by saying that she was now clearer about what she needed to do and that she felt good about it.

During our next session, Silvia's voice was very different. Her job situation still seemed very challenging, albeit somewhat clearer, but more importantly she felt that she was back on track with her Chinese team. I asked her what she had done: she had invested a substantial amount of time on a one-to-one basis with each member of the team. She told me

> *"Talking about food and cooking worked like a miracle: I actually found a good way to connect with two of them".*

She also mentioned that one team member sent her a special stone with a symbolic meaning, and how touched she was by this personal gesture. She then said:

> *"You know, I realised the mistake I made when I was under pressure: instead of discussing the latest figures I could have achieved so much more by starting my conversation with them talking about the snow that we already have here in Sweden".*

We both reflected further on the importance of this relationship work, and how quickly it was actually possible to rebuild these relationships that had seemed to be broken in the summer. We agreed on the fragility of these virtual relationships, but recognised at the same time how quickly they bounced back after Silvia's renewed efforts.

In my research Silvia exemplifies clearly the role of what I would like to call 'the relationship builder' in virtual leadership. This behaviour has become an obvious and inherent part of herself. At the end of that same year she explained to me that she now had an Indian member in her team, and I was impressed and pleased at the same time to hear the clarity of her plans to introduce him to the team, starting at a very personal level with the relation-ship building aspects. She had already reflected on how she perceived his personality (she had not met him face-to-face), what she anticipated would be easy and what might be more difficult for her Chinese colleagues, and how she wanted to go about dealing with that in her role of relationship builder.

Virtual popcorn meetings

The theme of relationship building has also been an important aspect of William's virtual leadership. As soon as he started transferring a significant amount of his leadership activities to the virtual space, he noticed the urgent need to do something at a personal level. Relatively early on he came up with the idea of 'virtual popcorn time', which he implemented with what he felt was a good result. He would organise teleconferences with no agenda. On a Friday afternoon, people would be invited into the conference and encour-aged to bring something to drink and nibble. The purpose of the meeting was to talk about things people wanted to talk about. This could be what had happened in the last two weeks, rumours, how people were feeling, etc.

William made a point of not bringing any agenda item and just being part of the conversation. He mentioned that when he started, people were a bit unsure and found the practice unusual, so at first not many attended. However, after a few virtual popcorn sessions, as the news spread that this was really good time spent together more and more people attended. Additionally, William would call specific members of his team individually, when he felt that they had made a point during one of the virtual meetings which he might not have answered to their (or certainly to his) satisfaction.

He told me how positively surprised people were to receive his call and hear him say:

"You know the point you made at our last virtual meeting? I am not sure that I answered it completely and I wanted to follow up on this with you", etc.

William had always been convinced that this would make a big difference, at least to his feeling of connectedness with his team. He also reflected with me on how different this type of activity would be from the face-to-face: in the latter you would not need to plan for this to happen, you would meet the person in the corridor and talk to them. Virtually, these calls would need to be planned and done on a regular basis, and they would require a lot of his time. During one of our conversations William actually mentioned how much he had noticed the shift in his activities, and how much more time he was spending in these relationship-building activities compared with the previous face-to-face situation.

Learning myself from the power of William's virtual popcorn time, I happened to mention this in a virtual session with a group of virtual leaders at InterCo, when they were expressing their concerns that relationships could only be built 'personally', by which they meant 'face-to-face'. This choice of language to describe 'face-to-face' as opposed to virtual (which as a consequence cannot be personal in their minds) is something which I have come across a lot in my work with virtual leaders. I challenged the automatic way in which they seemed to associate face-to-face and personal as opposed to virtual. There was a considerable silence on the line from the 14 participants, but I could feel that the silence was pregnant with intense thinking.

After a while, a few people started saying: 'Actually why not?' I then invited them to discuss in pairs how virtual popcorn time could look in their own teams and a few different ideas were discussed. To my delight, in a follow-up session with one of the participants, a lady in charge of leading several teams across the whole Asia region, revealed that she had been implementing 'virtual coffee corners' bi-weekly. She was really pleased with the results, and claimed that she would never have been able to implement the necessary changes in Asia without these virtual coffee corner conversations, because they were the emotional glue which kept the teams together.

I would like to come back to the common assumption, held implicitly rather than explicitly, that virtual working cannot be personal. In my experience of numerous conversations with leaders around this question, one key reason is the fact that people believe that, without seeing the person's eyes and body language, it is difficult to enter into a personal relationship with somebody. I have already written about the myth of body language (see Invitation 2). I will also come back to this aspect from another perspective when exploring the topic of trust in the virtual space (Invitation 6). Another interesting aspect that might explain people's difficulty in being able to imagine how personal relationships can develop virtually is illustrated through Sten's story.

The voices in Sten's ear

During one of our sessions I asked Sten this question:

> "Could you imagine leading a team of people without seeing them face-to-face for over a year?"

Sten answered immediately with a clear 'No'. I asked why, and he explained that he needed to see people physically for them to be real to him. I then invited him to explore how real B (a member of his team) was for him. He had been talking about her a lot, explaining that she needed a lot of attention in the virtual space and lots of support because of her very demanding job. B was taking a lot of Sten's time even though he did not see her often. So I asked:

> "Is B not real then? Would she be less real in those moments when she calls you to share her anger or frustration if you hadn't met her before?"

There was a short pause, and then Sten responded:

> "Actually I could manage her even if I had never seen her before. In these moments she is very real to me. I could do it, I guess. After a while it wouldn't matter to me any longer [whether I had met her or not]".

At this stage I was struck by how much Sten had moved in his thinking during a ten minute period. At the time I asked myself whether this was solely due to the fact that he had not stopped to think about this previously, or whether there was something else behind it that I ought to explore a bit more. I made a note of this in my papers.

Two months later, during my next conversation with Sten, I asked him whether we could return to this point, as it felt important for my/our inquiry.

Sten agreed, and through the meandering of our new conversation we suddenly focused on how and whether he praised B for her good work. He explained that he kept praise for occasions when they met face-to-face, and since they did not meet very often he felt that, as a result, he did not praise her enough. I then asked him whether he never gave praise during his virtual communications. He answered that he did, via email, at times, but that this was not enough. I asked him whether he would consider praising B during his phone conversations. Sten explained that the conversations tended to be task-focused:

"I cannot detach myself from the task".

I asked him why he thought that he behaved like that. I noticed a moment of silence and sensed some kind of embarrassment:

"I think this is because of the way I was brought up. I do the same at home. I ask Emily [Sten's daughter] to get off the phone when she talks for too long with her boyfriend".

This example shows nicely how some of us still associate phone calls with something expensive, hence the calls should be limited to what is 'important'.

The virtual leader as relationship builder

I want to come back to our starting point, namely Silvia's frustration, and even anger, towards members of her management team who could not understand the importance of building relationships if one wanted to succeed in leading virtually. We started by realising that, in a predominantly face-to-face leadership paradigm, the focus would be on processes and structures, and most of the time relationships would operate as the necessary oil in the machine and would develop as a by-product in the informal space. They would be an invisible 'given'.

In the virtual space, because relationships cannot develop if they are not given time, space, attention and care, they might end up being neglected and the leadership and/or management machine will not work: the oil is missing. However for most leaders starting to lead virtually, the sheer concept of building relationships virtually to support their work is challenging to say the least. Several implicit judgements get in the way. Nevertheless, as I hope I illustrate through my inquiries, relationships are essential.

Leaders who understand themselves as 'relationship builders' achieve amazing results. As a matter of fact when his organisation ran the yearly employee satisfaction survey William obtained significantly better results from his team than his colleagues, who were still leading in the traditional way, primarily through face-to-face meetings (albeit with reduced frequency since the organisation had cut travel costs) and this in spite of major uncertainties and on-going changes in the company.

To complete this section on the importance of relationships in virtual leadership I would like to mention the article 'The impact of superior–subordinate relationships on the commitment, job satisfaction, and performance of virtual workers' by Golden and Veiga (2008). Both authors claim that no analysis of the importance of the superior-subordinate relationships in the virtual space has been done so far. Through their work, based on a survey with 375 professional employees, they demonstrated how pivotal this relationship is, and its impact on commitment, job satisfaction and performance. They claim that traditional working relationships will need to change in the virtual space, although they remain unclear as to exactly how. From my research with my co-inquirers I would absolutely agree with them, and add that these relationships would need, at the outset, to be recognised as pivotal by leaders, and focused on intensively and worked on in a personal and dedicated way.

So what?

- You cannot have a virtual coffee, but you can have a coffee virtually with several people from around the world.

- You will not meet people in the corridors of cyberspace by coincidence. However you can plan for relationship-building activities in your agenda in the same way as you would plan budget meetings. Go through your calendar and check: 'How many hours have I spent this week building and nurturing relationships in the virtual space? How many hours have I got planned for this purpose for next week?'

- Be prepared to manage your boss's and colleagues' expectations and perceptions, since it might be difficult for them to understand why you spend so many hours on the phone or in front of your laptop with your headset on.

INVITATION 5
The Virtual Leader Is a 'Facileader'

In this section I will show that leading effectively virtually requires one (or several) people to feel responsible for leading. In the virtual space this also means facilitating in a wide and complex sense, paying as much attention to the process as the content. It also includes highly conscious choices regarding the medium to use and how to use it. This in turn requires skills and competencies that need to be learned and developed in people.

I want to explore different aspects of leading in the virtual space, in particular by looking into specific moments of leading virtually with the different leaders and participants I have accompanied during my research as well as in my consulting work. At the end of the section I will offer a summary of my findings regarding the role(s) of a virtual leader.

The MilkCo leaders' experience
The interviews with the MilkCo leaders brought up a very interesting theme around the actual concept of leadership. Going through my notes I notice the flurry of words used by my interviewees when describing the leadership aspects of the 'virtual strategy process': chairman, facilitator, leader, rotating leadership, rotating chairmanship, distributed leadership.

The patterns that actually emerged from the five teams over time (they worked for four months, only virtually, and were coached by myself and two colleagues) were very interesting. Although the leadership took several different forms across the teams, there were also some similarities.

The teams went for a variety of 'leadership formulae':
- One team went for a rotating leadership, where a different member of the team would lead for one meeting and all the time until the next meeting

- Three teams went for one leader taking responsibility for the team throughout the whole process
- One team went for what I would call a 'tandem-leadership', with one person leading the process in between the meetings (preparing, taking notes, and even making things happen) while another would 'chair' (their words) the meetings.

In spite of these different formulae there was recognition across all teams that this leadership required qualities which they described as follows:

"The chairman was not driving the meeting. It was about keeping it together".

"The idea was that there was no leader but a rotating chairman, also in between the meetings".

"The leadership was about securing that there was an agenda, that objectives were reached, taking the responsibility of leading for four hours".

"I would not give myself the label of 'leader'. It was distributed. I was contributing to pushing the project forward, putting things in writing, developing a shared understanding, getting structure into the thoughts. It was about providing a careful process to develop a shared understanding and not leaving anything unsaid".

"The leader as an enabler, not the one putting his view forward".

"X was serving the team".

"As a good virtual leader he showed himself as a facilitator. He was the one who put himself in the service of the virtual team".

"You want to deliver. You want to be ahead of the group in order to provide the group with security, safety, comfort, a feeling of reliance. However you don't impose. You only ask questions".

"To take the lead you have to be more careful".

"The risk of failing (in the sense of not being accepted) is much bigger than in face-to-face". "[...] it is different from the face-to-face, in that it is not about leading by taking decisions, or telling the way, but what is key is the agenda, clear goals, ensuring participation from everyone all the time. Preparation is essential [...]. For me a pivotal moment in the group was when I provided an

action plan. This helped the group to move forward". [...] "I established my leadership by providing a structure and a plan".

"The leader is mainly a facilitator. His opinion is not more important than the opinion of others. It is about being extremely careful, repeating, checking the understanding, giving verbal clues".

"It puts a lot of pressure on the chairman: preparing the agenda, leading the meeting, facilitating".

"The leader is a virtual facilitator. When facilitating you need to be very alert, listening, leading, shifting the focus of your concentration from process to content".

"It was Y leading after a while [...]. She was driving the process although others were actively leading as well, but it was good to have an elected leader as fallback, for the cases when others get stuck. It is a different leadership".

There are two examples in particular which illustrate how the team members came to the realisation that a different type of leadership was needed, compared with what they already knew. I will take the examples of Team 4 (which I was coaching) and Team 5 (which a colleague was coaching). In both teams the members had taken great care up front to discuss and decide who should be the leader of the team. They felt that they had come to a good decision. However in Team 4 they soon came to realise that the way they worked was not going well. The official leader of the team remembers:

"We were desperately looking for a line; there were so many different angles [to the issue]. We were getting stuck".

I asked him: 'What made the shift for you?'. He answered:

"I realised that I had to prepare for the meetings much more and to work on something that we could discuss".

Another interviewee from the same team explained:

"Z was serving the team. He understood quickly ... that he needed to adapt".

What happened in Team 5 was similar. The team leader remembers:

"After the first meeting with me leading I realised that I had not prepared enough. I didn't know what to expect [...]. I had underestimated the difference between leading a meeting face-to-face and virtually. During the first meeting we had a silence. It felt like emptiness. The leadership was unclear [...]. We

decided that someone else needed to take the lead, and it was a smooth process. We had some dips during the project but there was always somebody to pick us up. We all had respect for each other's leadership".

These two stories illustrate well that even when they had clearly agreed on who should be the leader, the team members were not clear about the kind of leadership needed in this virtual process. They had to discover this as they went along. In each of these teams something went wrong – or at least they got stuck. From a phenomenological perspective, the difficulty obliged the team members to move from a 'ready-to-hand' to a 'present-at-hand' awareness (Ladkin 2010); this means that they were confronted with the need to deal with the very nature of the (their) leadership in the team, and that they could not just transfer on to this virtual process what they would automatically do face-to-face.

The process of regular reflection helped them to do this. In both cases one key learning was that they needed to prepare before and follow up better after the meeting. In other words they had to become less event and more process focused in terms of flow of information, tasks and relationships. In the end Team 4 went for one leader throughout the whole process while Team 5, as mentioned before, decided to go for a 'rotating leadership'. Both ended up having different experiences, and these too provide important learning and insights.

I interviewed five of the six members of Team 5, and four of the five members of Team 4. While all these teams members mentioned to me how energised they felt by the work, and how much everybody was 'pulling their weight' – confirmed by my colleague Peter who was coaching Team 5 – Team 4 seems to have had a slightly different experience. My interviewees from that Team all underlined that they felt responsible for the team results, and that they had ownership of the team work, given the leadership style of their team leader who enabled others to take leadership. In my role as coach to the team I actually witnessed this. However, the team leader himself at times felt rather overloaded with the leading task, and perceived it as very energy consuming:

"I felt the need to be better prepared than the rest [...]. I took on too much. It was probably due to my own very high motivation. If I had not been so motivated, I would not have taken on too much. [...] I had the fear that it would fall apart if I didn't give it backbone. It was my own anxiety: what if nobody takes the baby?"

I could certainly observe how much the team leader was taking on during the project, and twice I even offered him my observation about this. There was a need to give structure to something that felt unbounded and unstructured. Interestingly, if I look at my inquiry with William I note that in the beginning he also defined his virtual leadership in these terms, focusing on providing structure and stability.

The experience of Team 2 at MilkCo also seems to echo this:

"Nothing happened until one of us took the lead. [...] When leading, you feel fully responsible. It [the responsibility] is on your table" (leader of Team 2).

Another member of Team 2 explained that there was a lack of leadership in the team:

"Nobody wanted to take the lead. [...] the team leader had to take on a big role. Delegation of leadership to others was difficult. Nobody knew how to tackle this [leadership] issue".

Does this mean that a rotating leadership is a better approach in helping avoid over-reliance patterns? Or does it mean that the leader of a virtual team needs to find ways to care well for the team without making the team members feeling that they are being too compliant and dependent? Also, what about the potential lack of leadership that might occur in a virtual team?

There is still little literature about the leadership of virtual teams. The few authors who talk about the leadership aspects do not directly mention the concept of 'rotating leadership', but argue that 'distributed leadership' (which I consider close to 'rotating leadership' in the sense that the leadership does not rely on the same person all the time) correlates positively with virtual teams' performance. They quickly associate virtual teams with self-managing teams. For example Yoo and Alavi (2003), who did a longitudinal study of the email exchange of seven ad-hoc and temporary virtual teams of senior executives in the US, suggest that future research conceptualises virtual team leadership as 'distributed leadership'. The same applies to Bell and Kozlowski (2002), who developed a rather complicated typology of virtual teams, and concluded that because leaders of virtual teams cannot directly monitor team members, they need to create self-managing teams with distributed leadership.

In the light of my research findings I do not agree with these conclusions. The MilkCo leaders in particular understood a lot about self-managing teams, as they had worked in such project teams several times before, but this did not necessarily help them in this process.

It is perhaps no coincidence that in the literature, until recently hardly anybody has spoken about virtual leadership in virtual teams because, as we have seen, leading virtually might be more about facilitating (which would require researchers to think in new and shifting categories); at the same time, it seems more difficult for people to step up and take a lead in the virtual space, as they don't know up front what leading virtually actually means. Leaders might feel intuitively that leading virtually is different from what they have known as leadership so far, and therefore be scared or intimidated by the fact that they don't know how different it will be and what this difference is about.

Another interesting angle on the issue of virtual leadership was provided by the opinion of one member of Team 3. The interviewee completely shared the view that, based on her experience of the 'virtual strategy process' at MilkCo, leading successfully in the virtual space meant first facilitating virtual team work. However, she was also very clear that the virtual leader could not at the same time facilitate the meeting (in the sense of focusing on the process, listening, being alert to and identifying people's emotions) as well as putting across his/her own views. I invited her to explore this strong view in more detail with me. She talked about her own experience in the team when she took on the facilitation role, and explained that it is very hard – almost impossible – to focus intensively on the process and on the content at the same time, and to do justice to both. We both came to the conclusion that this requires great versatility and that the leader ought to be able to shift focus swiftly between process and content.

This line of thought also resonated very much with my own experience, and I would like to make a small diversion here to underline this aspect.

When facilitating the virtual workshop with my Doctoral peers, Cindy, who already had experience of working virtually with groups, noticed the richness of the WebEx platform:

> "We can all simultaneously chat with each other, speak with each other in plenary and co-create or write things together on the whiteboard. In the face-to-face environment we would usually be able to do only one at a time".

Cindy wondered:

> "If we are to become practised in tapping into the richness of all these forms..".

The moment that she said it I noticed my head vehemently nodding, and my mind immediately reconnected with previous thoughts about that: indeed if we were to develop the capacity to communicate at all these levels simultaneously, what might such an experience be like? I assume that we would need to let go even more of our linear way of thinking and interacting with each other, as different streams of interaction and communication might go on simultaneously with the same people and/or different people, and the sense-making process might become more cyclical, or more something else (I can't even imagine the form it might take at this stage).

However, in the workshop I limited myself (more unconsciously than consciously) to reacting to Cindy's thoughts by underlining the choices that I felt I needed to make as a facilitator, knowing that I cannot at the same time attend to what is going on in the audio space, on the whiteboard and in the chat room.

I answered that I sometimes

"get overwhelmed by this. I constantly need to make choices. My brain cannot get it all".

This has actually been an ongoing challenge during all the virtual events that I have facilitated. For example, when I was facilitating a strategic engagement process with a major global organisation (RasCo) I noticed that during the online workshops the participants had a tendency either to speak a lot (taking a lot of air time) or write a lot in the chat room. I have observed myself in these instances taking a quick look at the chat room now and again, and inviting the people who posted something there to share it orally with the other participants, though they might have wanted to avoid this in the first place. But confronted with my own limitation of comprehending all the different streams of sense-making going on at the same time, I assume that the same must be going on for the participants, and certainly for the ones in a leading position within the team.

So what might be different ways of communicating, facilitating and leading that might combine these parallel streams of thought in a more natural way? Are we here encountering the opportunity to develop new skills for a richer sense-making experience? If the leader or facilitator of a meeting does not attempt to bring into the audio, and hence the plenary conversation, the exchange happening in the chat room, would this reinforce the disconnection between the formal discussion (in the audio/plenary) and the informal (in the chat room)? What might be the consequences of that in terms of the team's dynamics and performance?

Before moving on with my questions about leadership forms in the virtual space, I want to pause and underline one specific aspect: you might have noticed, particularly in the last paragraph, that I constantly move from 'leader' to 'facilitator' (or from 'facilitating' to 'leading') and vice-versa in my questions. I feel that it is important to do so as a way of going in deeper and stretching the semantics.

At this point, Alvesson's views on leadership research are relevant:

"An open attitude to the subject matter, including considerations of alternative research vocabularies or lines of interpretation before, during or after the research process (Alvesson & Sköldberg, forthcoming; Rorty, 1989), may benefit the intellectual inquiry" (Alvesson 1996, p.469).

Coming back to MilkCo and my interviewee from Team 3, as soon as we came to the tentative conclusion that there was a need for a new profile of a virtual leader, she bounced back and explained that she did not believe that this was the solution either – assuming that it would be possible for a virtual leader to develop the skills and capabilities of such versatile leading. In her view, the moment a leader puts across his/her own standpoint on an issue s/he would immediately lose his/her credibility as a facilitator. According to her, there is something so fragile and at the same time so important in the leadership-facilitation aspect that it can be destroyed quickly if the person in charge of the meeting tries to push his/her opinion. Therefore she was strongly advocating a clear separation of facilitating and taking a standpoint. I should stress that this view was in some aspects already present in the words of one member of Team 4, who specified that the leader of a virtual team had to put him/herself at the service of the team.

The consequences of this standpoint would be twofold: either the leader (in the traditional sense of chairing a meeting, stating his/her standpoint and taking decisions) would need to get a facilitator for his meetings in the virtual space, or the concept of leadership in the virtual space would need to shift altogether, with leading becoming more about enabling, serving, and providing the space for others to work and decide. In any case it would be a space where leading and facilitating became blurred.

These consequences would be true for the synchronous (see glossary) mode, but how would they look in the asynchronous (see glossary) mode? While I can easily see the leading-facilitating tandem formula working well in the synchronous – this view is based on my experience of the 'virtual strategy process' at MilkCo as well as my own general experience as a consultant – I find it more difficult to imagine how the scenario of the leader in the traditional sense with an additional facilitator would work as well in the asynchronous space, for example when it comes to scheduling and preparing for virtual meetings, keeping virtual relationships going on a one-on-one basis, answering individual questions, monitoring the performance of the individual team members, keeping the team informed, etc. Does this mean that one person would look only at the process in the asynchronous mode, while another would make sense of the content, take decisions and communicate these? Does it mean that both would work in tandem on a continuous basis? How sustainable is this in the long term? Also what might the implications be of delegating the process aspects to a single person in the virtual space? Would virtual leaders (the ones taking decisions) ever become able to lead virtually on their own if they do not develop this virtual process competence?

Actually the experience of Team 3 might support, at least partially, the concept of a leadership tandem. As a coach of Team 3, I experienced early in the work how the team members became stuck. Asking the official team leader what he felt got him/them 'stuck' elicited the answer:

"We had the discussion about me taking on the leadership. We should really have discussed what that means – 'leader' – in that context".

He thus expressed the same idea of a new, or at least different, understanding of what 'leading' meant. I then asked him what he felt got him/them 'unstuck' and he answered:

"The big difference was when we talked about the way we worked together, and we divided work [...]. It was because we had the discussion and we organised the work among ourselves. Everyone contributed in several ways. [...] the leadership was discussed, and we made real progress".

Team 3 went for a tandem solution with one person facilitating the meetings and the other preparing and making things happen in between. The division of roles was not between leading (in the sense of taking a standpoint and making decisions) and facilitating the virtual meetings, but it was still a division between two roles, facilitating synchronously (role A) and managing and facilitating asynchronously (role B), both roles together making an effective virtual leadership.

The reflections from and with my interviewees so far do not seem to point to a clear 'winning formula' in terms of virtual leadership. However they certainly show what worked and what did not work in the specific circumstances of the 'virtual strategy process', even with the differences between teams. There is also the clear recognition that, whatever leadership formula each team opted for, none corresponded with the traditional view of leadership.

The concrete examples of virtual leadership experienced by the teams certainly raise important and interesting questions. The key one for me at this stage is whether the scope of leading virtually is too wide for only one person to take on (as this would require a considerable capability to embrace and shift swiftly between content and process), or whether it would be possible to develop the skills and capabilities of virtual leaders so that they can take on this bigger scope individually.

At this point I also want to pause and reflect on the new emerging category of virtual leadership as a blurred area between the traditional categories of leading and facilitating. Ladkin (2010) underlines how important it is for the leadership researcher to be aware of the 'absences'. By the concept of 'absences' she means the invisible factors influencing what occurs, what people expect of their leaders, what leaders expect of their teams, etc. as a result of their background.

"In summary, one cause of the difficulties associated with studying leadership is that as a socially constructed phenomenon, it operates largely through its absence. This includes the absent expectations carried by both the 'leader' and the 'followers', through the stories that are told about the 'leader' and through the culture from which leadership arises". (Ladkin 2010, p.43)

I am very aware that MilkCo is a Swedish company, and that the Swedishness of the leadership is dominant in the organisation worldwide. In Swedish organisations, in my experience, leaders are generally expected to take on an enabling and coaching leadership approach rather than a prescribing, heroic approach. Nevertheless my experience of the organisation over the previous three years had been that leaders would still present their views while seeking to achieve some consensus through a facilitative process in the decision making. Thus they would not limit themselves to being pure facilitators in the traditional leadership space.

However, I now wonder whether the fact that my interviewees so clearly emphasise the importance of serving the team and facilitating, corresponds to an 'absence' (Ladkin 2010), in other words to what one would expect from a leader in a Swedish company in any circumstances. This 'absence' regarding the facilitative aspect of leadership expected by the MilkCo leaders would become pretty loud and present in their interpretation of their experience of the 'virtual strategy process' through our inquiry process, and would therefore influence their conclusion as to what makes effective virtual leadership.

Another way to approach this question would be to ask: 'Would I have achieved similar results if MilkCo had been an American or a French company?'. Actually it seems that virtual working is currently more widespread in the Scandinavian countries than anywhere else in Europe. In the context of my work at Ashridge I also notice that of the four key projects that we delivered in virtual working / virtual leadership between 2007 and 2008, three were for Scandinavian companies (this trend also carries on until today, albeit with more German and US-based companies entering the stage).

Therefore another conclusion could be that precisely because Scandinavian leadership cultures tend more towards a facilitative stance, they seem to be more disposed to leading virtually. Obviously another interpretation could be that Scandinavian countries are usually much more aware of environmental concerns, and therefore Scandinavian leaders and managers are more willing and open to the challenges of leading virtually. It could also be a combination of both reasons.

The notion of blurred categories of leadership linked with the difficulty of leading in the virtual space is, I believe, a very central one. Therefore I would like to persevere for a bit longer and bring in the results from my collaborative inquiry group (involving two British, one German and myself as French) which, although they emerged initially from a different perspective, actually arrive at the same conclusions.

Unwillingness to lead

I was keen to engage with Barbara, Matthew and Silvia, the members of my collaborative inquiry group, in a truly collaborative way for this research. Therefore for me it was important that we would take turns to lead the process, in terms of getting together virtually, preparing our session, leading the session, etc. I saw my role as setting the stage, agreeing on issues such as confidentiality, the research question and methodology, but beyond that I was planning and hoping that somebody else in the group would take the lead. I suggested this in the second session and to my big surprise, and also my genuine disappointment, my three co-researchers refused to take the lead. I asked why and they answered that they felt leading the session might get in the way of their learning.

To some extent I could understand their response – interestingly, more at an instinctive than a rational level – and I decided not to inquire further into it. At my next doctoral supervision session I took the opportunity to tell my story of the collaborative inquiry group, and was encouraged to bring the question back to the group. In the following two sessions I was carried away by the richness of our conversations; I was so excited about the real issues that my co-researchers were bringing into our work that, although I made a note to raise the question as an agenda item beforehand, I never actually asked it. I had an instinct, maybe a fear, that this might change the dynamics in the group, which I perceived as being really good. My co-researchers in the group also confirmed these good dynamics.

Nevertheless during the last session I resolved to explore this question with the group as a way of concluding our reflection on how we felt we worked together, and as a way of learning about virtual leadership directly through our lived experience together. The conversation that my question generated again proved to be a very rich one. I asked the question in a rather provocative way, talking about 'your unwillingness to lead' and inviting my co-researchers to explain why this was so, and this produced the following reactions:

Silvia: "For me it was pure luxury not to lead, not feeling the responsibility for the facilitation of others in the group because I have enough of this to do in the [Silvia's] team".

Matthew: "For me it would have changed the nature of the relationship between us in the group. We are a group of equals. This would have changed the nature of interactions between us. This highlights the requirement to think very well how you structure virtual teams".

Barbara: "I do it every day. This was vacation. One part of not wanting to do it was about wanting to take the time of enjoying you [Ghislaine] and your way of running the sessions. I wanted to see it as learning and not working".

While Barbara's and Silvia's answers were very clear to me, I wanted to inquire further into Matthew's views and asked: 'Would it also have changed the nature of the relationships between you if you had gone for a rotating leadership?'

Both Matthew and Silvia answered without hesitation: 'Yes!' I then went on to ask: 'Does this mean that the concept of rotating leadership, or even distributed leadership, doesn't work in the virtual space for you?'

Matthew answered:

"This is not quite right: we were all leading informally at different parts of the conversations. We all took the leadership".

Silvia reacted vividly to this:

"Still for me you [Ghislaine] were the formal leader. The overall responsibility for the results of the process was with you. We were 3+1".

Barbara was clearly agreeing with Silvia:

"This [the fact that you were the 'formal' leader] didn't stop us from leading. We did not lose power. I expected us to be 3+1. This was not a surprise and I am not sure how comfortable it would have left me otherwise".

We then continued to reflect on the nature of the role I took, and underlined the importance of the leader providing a structure, an agenda, serving the group, etc. We can see here a similarity with one outcome brought up in the inquiry strand with the MilkCo leaders. Suddenly Matthew reacted: *'That's a facilitator to me!'* To which I responded by asking: 'And how does this sit with you, Matthew, and the way you see yourself when you lead your Indian team virtually?' Matthew answered:

"That's absolutely fine for me because I see my job as facilitating for others to do their job. You need to take more care about it in the virtual space. You need to have the skill set. Call it what you want: facilitating, facilitative leadership ..".

Silvia very much agreed with Matthew, and at the same time underlined that this concept of facilitation in the virtual space would also need to include the notion of responsibility for the results, and cannot only imply the more traditional concept of process facilitation. Matthew and Silvia then got into synch by claiming: 'This is a responsible facilitator.'

Barbara, who had been quieter – more in the background – joined in:

"I see a need to be extra mindful. Are you leading? Are you facilitating? [...] In my job I need to do both. Virtually the need to facilitate is even heavier, clearer".

Matthew came very naturally to the concept of facilitator as we were reflecting on the leadership in our inquiry group, and automatically saw this concept also applying to his role in the virtual space... as did Silvia and Barbara. This seems to correlate strongly with the views of the MilkCo managers. I also want to uphold the concept of 'the responsible facilitator' which I find helpful, in the sense that the facilitator not only holds the responsibility for the process but also for the results and decisions s/he might take.

For Silvia and Barbara, leading in our group would have been an additional load that they did not wish to take on, preferring to learn from our process and enjoy it. I see a parallel with my inquiry with the MilkCo managers, as for most of them leading in the virtual space was a task that nobody really wanted to take on. In the case of MilkCo I interpreted the reason to be mainly linked with the fact that they did not really know what leading virtually meant. However Barbara and Silvia were experienced, yet deliberately chose not to take the role, because it would have meant more work, more effort, more responsibility. In other words I see an emerging pattern (common for MilkCo and my inquiry group) that the art of leading virtually is a difficult one and hard work, requiring a lot of effort, care and attention. In one of the previous sessions Matthew explained why, in his view, there are still so few people who really lead virtually and why so many others are still dependent on the face-to-face:

"Unless you put a lot of effort into it, the difference of outcomes with the face-to-face is beyond comparison".

Finally I also want to notice and underline the dance between the words that my co-inquirers were using and how often they moved from *leading* to *facilitating* and from *facilitating* to *leading* revealing some kind of shifting concept in their minds.

William's emerging new leadership

William's example also seems to point in the direction of the leader acting as facilitator as well, although William never used the word 'facilitator' as such, and I never prompted him to comment on this notion. Nevertheless the list of activities that William undertook would certainly account for a leader responsible for achieving results as well as facilitating virtual meetings and actually 'designing' them.

In our sessions, as a way to help him reflect on his progress and learning, I always asked him to tell me about his activities and to describe his virtual meetings. William often organised, for example, virtual town halls, using a mixture of people face-to-face and connected via screens across the plants (not with cameras, but a screen showing information, pictures, etc.). He also organised purely virtual meetings with his team, as well as virtual action learning sessions with his direct reports as a way to encourage learning from each other across the plants. While he still saw his responsibility as commenting on the results and current developments in the organisation, setting goals and reaffirming the vision for his department, he would also in the virtual space, pay minute attention to questions such as:

- Should I be alone and linked into the plants only virtually or should I be with one group in one plant and rotate between the plants?

- Should I be together with my management team or should each member of my management team be in a separate location?

- How much information should I share?

- Which process should I select to invite questions? Who would be best placed to answer these, and how?

- How shall I create a feeling of community across the plants?

- What symbols would be important to me?

In each of our virtual sessions William would spend a substantial amount of time telling me what he did, what he learnt, what he thought of doing differently next time. In his activities as a virtual leader he also engaged one member of his team, Maria, who had expertise in communication, asking her to develop with him the plan for the next virtual event. He relentlessly experimented with the questions above and slowly defined his own way to lead his team virtually.

Once William told me that he was 'punished' (his word) for not having prepared well enough for a virtual meeting. Prior to the virtual town hall he had asked his team members to send him a list of their achievements throughout the year so far. He explained to me that his aim was to acknowledge and thank everybody for their contribution, in spite of an extremely difficult situation in the organisation, but also that he wanted to do this by putting the emphasis on team achievement rather than individuals. He chose to show a bunch of flowers where each flower, linked to a list of the achievements of an individual, would be pretty but would become even more beautiful in the context of the bunch. William felt very disappointed:

"People didn't get it. They all looked for what they did individually. I was lacking the WE. I realised that I didn't spend enough time preparing for this meeting, the choice of messages and how I wanted to engage my team".

We discussed what exacting preparation this type of virtual meeting would require: William felt that he needed much more care, detailed thinking and focus for the preparation of virtual meetings than for face-to-face ones.

However, William was happy with another experiment. As another way to celebrate achievements he had organised for similar cakes to be delivered at the same time in each of the plants that were connected virtually. William said that this was a great success and he felt that people connected emotionally with each other across geographies when eating the cake together across the plants. I could feel that William was really pleased with himself. Several tones were present in his voice. The rhythm of his words was light and sustained. I asked him: 'Do you have a sense of why these cakes made such a difference?'

He was not sure. Listening to him I had the clear sense of a moment of communion that William had been facilitating across geographies. I shared this thought with him and his reaction was:

"You must be right. This was exactly how it felt. It was a real moment of sharing and being together!"

I was absolutely delighted because William told me that now he was really feeling that his own role and style of leading virtually were becoming clear to him: for example the use of music to create a common emotional platform across the plants had become a fact of life for all in the team (see details about the use of music in Invitation 8):

"It was funny at the beginning; now we don't question it any longer".

Now he was developing his own ideas and experimenting with them.

Behind all this minute thinking and planning William had been very clear from an early stage that he wanted to create a community of learning and best practice across the six different plants, in spite of, or because of, their remoteness. All this time he had been reflecting with me on his role in doing this. When we talked later on, he was not only happy but proud. He had just received the results of the annual employee survey: he had the best results. His direct reports and the second line gave 82% level of satisfaction with his communication and leadership as opposed to his peers – the next one was 75%. In spite of leading his team mostly virtually, William got better results than his colleagues who led their teams predominantly face-to-face. However, William mentioned the shadow side of these fantastic results: at the next level down in the organisation William got only 65% as opposed to the average of his peers at around 75%. William explained to me that these results showed that while, despite leading virtually, he got far better results from his direct reports, he had neglected the levels further down the organisation. He shared his frustration:

"I want to engage my direct reports and the second line more in leading their own teams virtually, but this is really hard work".

Over a period of almost a year William had been facilitating virtual action learning sessions with his management, hoping that they would in turn bring into the organisation this way of working and learning together. However, with the exception of two managers in his team, the others had not been proactive so far. William was now exploring with me what he could do to create this virtual community of learning as best practice across the plants. He then expressed the following:

"I feel that I am working on my own [at leading virtually]. It feels like a dark cloud".

William said that he only had the support of Maria, his assistant with communication expertise. I asked him exactly what he expected from his direct reports and the next line:

"I want them to organise their own virtual action learning sessions with their teams and spread this way of working across the organisation; I want them to rethink the role of the hub managers in the plants in this context and to give more autonomy and a stronger positioning to this role".

I then asked him how he would like to achieve this and he answered with no hesitation that he wanted to have his managers 'trained' in virtual communication. William was clear, however, that there were currently no resources in the organisation to pay for an external coach.

At this stage William said something that felt really important:

"For me it is now about moving up the scale. I feel ready for a coaching role [he was planning to help his management team to become virtual leaders by coaching them]. I do think things over, I am on a steep learning curve but I am now ready to enable my managers to lead virtually".

At the end of our conversation I genuinely felt a huge sense of happiness and satisfaction: William was really becoming the virtual leader that he wanted to become. It was his own thing now and he was going with it.

Reflecting on the role that William had been shaping for himself, I would argue that he was combining his role of traditional leader (as the one following up on results, giving goals, setting a direction, etc) with the role of a facilitator of communication and learning across geographies (by minutely choosing his media, messages and communication processes) and the role of a coach. Although he never framed his role in this way, I would argue that this was very much what he had been experimenting with. For him leading and facilitating would not be an either/or, it would not be a simple combination either in the sense of 1+1, but more a specific mixture (his mixture) and a different, new category of leading. At the same time I could not refrain from noticing the 'dark cloud': his loneliness in pioneering this way of working in an organisation which, from tradition and through the type of products that they make and sell, is so bound up in the face-to-face. William is truly a conqueror of the virtual space.

Silvia's virtual leadership role

Another interesting example of virtual leading is that of Silvia. She had shared her view of her role as a facilitator in the context of the collaborative inquiry group, but I was keen to hear about it in more detail in the context of my coaching with her. Instead of discussing this aspect further on a one-to-one basis, I asked whether we could have a teleconference with one or more members of her Chinese team, and reflect about her role together. To my surprise she readily accepted this idea, seeing it as a real opportunity to consolidate learning for her and for her team. She suggested that we talked to F, a member of the Chinese team who was more senior than the others, because she felt that F would be more reflexive, and discussing these abstract aspects of leadership might be easier for him than for his colleagues.

I agreed carefully with her on the positioning of the teleconference as a way to reflect on what constitutes effective virtual leadership in their team, both in the context of my research and also in the hope that it would help the team. We crafted an invitation email to F. F, a Chinese person who had never worked abroad, had prepared himself very thoroughly for the teleconference.

This made it in some aspects more difficult for Silvia and me to get into a real inquiry mode, as he came with well thought-through answers. I decided to go with the flow. F's opinion about what made the virtual team successful was pretty clear:

> "There should be no leader. Everybody's voice is equal. Silvia is a good listener. She is holding the meeting. She is not the formal leader. It really needs effort".

He then made another very important point when I asked him why he felt that this required effort. He mentioned that the concept of a team with no formal leader did not correspond to the Chinese leadership and management culture in his team, but nevertheless he felt it was absolutely key that in order for a leader to lead effectively virtually they needed to act as a good facilitator/enabler/convenor, even in a culture tending to be hierarchical*.

The virtual leader as a facileader

The results shown in this section indicate that the boundaries between leading and facilitating are blurred when it comes to leading effectively virtually. Furthermore even the concept of facilitation itself does not necessarily correspond to what I could call the traditional understanding of facilitation, in the sense of focusing on the process of an event and enabling others to have the conversations that they need to have. It seems that facilitation in the virtual space might become more complex and involve detailed thinking about communication, choices of media, and working simultaneously on different levels, e.g. chatting with people while asking questions in the virtual plenary, and co-creating documents on the virtual platform as well as bearing responsibility for the outcomes of the work. In other words even the definition of the leader as an enabler (Katzenbach and Smith, 1993) would not sufficiently cover the complexity of activities and competencies needed and described in this chapter.

Stacey's (1992) and Griffin's (2002) concept of self-organising teams, in which the individual leader emerges depending on his/her capability to deal with complexity and uncertainty, the on-going purpose and the task at hand, does not seem to be sufficient, as it misses the point of altogether new competencies being needed. I would argue that the question as to whether a team can self-organise virtually is very important and cannot be answered easily. Actually the examples above might hint at a negative answer to the question.

---

* F's statement regarding the leadership culture in China corresponds to what can be read in the interesting research by Cheng et al. (2004), who explore the concept of "Paternalistic Leadership" consisting of the following three elements: benevolence, morality and authoritarianism. Cheng et al explain that authoritarianism still exists in China but is in the process of disappearing in the light of modernisation.

There is a real need for dedicated leadership in the virtual space and this cannot be left to emergence.

It seems to me that there is a new category of intervention emerging in the virtual space, something that goes beyond a mere hybrid between leading and facilitating, requiring new awareness, new skills and competencies, and going far beyond the mere capacity to deal with a new communication technology.

I would apply the same caution to the claim of Joshi et al (2009) that inspirational leadership plays a crucial role in dispersed teams. I very much welcome their critical questioning of the frequently advocated concept of self-managed teams in the virtual space. While I also agree with their advocacy for the training of virtual leaders in a set of competencies specifying and associating behaviours and inspirational leadership, I would argue at the same time that this might not suffice in equipping leaders to lead effectively virtually.

My own claim at this stage is that effective virtual leadership requires a much more fundamental questioning of basics in terms of 'who I am' as a virtual leader and how I relate to others and the world, as well as the willingness to go beyond the existing categories and leadership frameworks developed from within a predominantly face-to-face paradigm.

It seems to me that leading in the virtual space requires from the leader that s/he makes it *easy* for the team members to engage with each other and to find new ways of relating with one another, given that the virtual space presents new parameters in terms of 'presence', 'here and now'. This would correspond to the notion of 'facilitation' in its original sense, namely from the Latin 'facilis' (easy) or the French 'faciliter' (to render easy)*. It is as if the leader has to *facil*-itate to enable others to relate and connect in this new space, and to lead at the same time by giving directions: the virtual leader as a '**facil**eader'?

---

* To facilitate: 1610s, from Fr. faciliter "to render easy," from L. facilis "easy" (see facile). Related: Facilitated; facilitates; facilitating. http://www.etymonline.com Online Etymology Dictionary

So what?

- Leading virtually is not easy and might cause you to feel lonely at times as only a few people will understand what you are attempting to do. This will probably equate to leading people through a real change process

- Leading virtually also means facilitating, without losing sight of your responsibility for the results

- Facilitating virtually means making it easy for the team members to work, relate, connect and think together in a space with its own idiosyncrasies

- Facilitating virtually means choosing the right media, choosing the right technology, making choices as to when to communicate on a one-to-one or on a team basis, and when to communicate synchro-nously or asynchronously (see Invitation 7 'Shape your virtual culture' for more details)

- Shift from an event-based way of leading to a process-based one by thinking ahead about what needs to be prepared and communicated upfront, and/or sent after the virtual meetings: what you do in-between the meetings is just as important as what you do during them!

- Experiment with the concept of **FACILEADING**

- You can find further practical hints and tips in Tool Box E

INVITATION 6
Your Power Is Trust!

In the virtual space the boundaries between trust and power become blurred: trust becomes power and power gets in the way of trust. Leaders will need to be highly reflexive in how they contribute to the development of trust in their virtual teams, and to question intensively their sources of power in those teams. These will be different from the power sources that they might be able to rely on in a face-to-face context.

In this section I intend to provide some idea of how the categories of trust and power might be shifting in the virtual space. While it has not been possible to reach final conclusions on both topics, the research offers the following starting points:

- Power in the virtual space depends on trust

- In the virtual space, development of trust is rather complex, but it can be developed purely virtually, contrary to what the predominant voices suggest: while this requires intense relational work it has the potential to yield highly powerful outcomes

- In the virtual space the semantic fields of trust and power are very rich and wide, and current research does not always do justice to this complexity. I believe that, for leaders to succeed in leading virtually, it will be essential to grapple with this complexity. High reflexivity (see glossary) will be essential to achieve this.

When trust becomes power

In the second session of our collaborative inquiry group, Matthew shared with us an interesting challenge that turned out to be a fascinating story for our learning.

Matthew explained that, in the context of his role as Accounting Director, he needed to develop a new accounting standard for the group across India, Europe and the US. He was currently facing what felt like a tough issue with the Indian team, with whom he was working virtually. Matthew is a very experienced virtual leader and has been leading virtually for several years. In spite of his experience, he explained that in this particular case:

"We talk a lot about the same issue and still it is very hard to ensure sufficient clarity and agree on what is required. [...] Although I do have many tools and methods to make this happen it doesn't happen. The methods that I have always used in the past are not working. Sometimes, after a virtual meeting, I feel that we are finally clear (about the issue); then two weeks later I find out that there is no clear shared understanding".

Barbara asked him: *'What is it that you are trying to achieve?'* Matthew answered:

"It is truly about co-creating something that needs to be accepted locally at the subsidiary level as well as at the global level of the whole organisation".

At this stage the whole group was working with Matthew in an action learning format, trying to help him to develop a different perspective on the issue. We explored with him the degree of complexity of the task; we also explored with him the type of leadership which he thought might be needed to achieve the task; we then went on to look at the cross-cultural challenges involved, as Matthew implemented new accounting standards across the US, Europe and India.

The more we explored the different aspects of the issue at hand, the clearer it became to me that Matthew had not only thought about all the issues but had also acted on them, unfortunately with no results. In spite of his calm, always composed manner, Matthew's frustration and near despair were resonating through the virtual space:

"This is one of the most difficult challenges I have ever had in my leadership [...] not being able to understand what is required is frustrating".

At this stage I felt that Barbara, Silvia and I were sharing the same sense of despair, as we were not sure how we could help any longer. The silence between us felt very full and heavy.

One of the aspects that remained unclear for me, and which sounded like an avenue that Matthew perhaps had not explored, was how the Indian team felt about the task, and how much time they had taken to discuss the ways they wanted to work together in the virtual space. From my previous experience of working virtually, as well as from several conversations I had with colleagues and leaders at the start of my inquiry, I believe that agreeing on the ways of working together is particularly important in the virtual space. Therefore I offered the question to Matthew, who became silent for a short while and then admitted that he had not taken the time to explore this. For a while we discussed these two aspects (the team feelings about the task and the potential discussion about ways of working together) and I could feel that Matthew was relaxing a bit and generating new energy. At the end of his slot, I asked him what he was going to do. He explained that he wanted to focus even more on the relationship with the team in India, and that he would start exploring some of the aspects linked to it with his main counterpart in the Indian organisation.

At the next session we were all keen to find out what had happened to Matthew and his issue. So as soon as we had reconnected with each other and completed our focus exercise (see Tool Box C) Matthew was asked to update the group. He shared the most amazing news with us. He did talk to his counterpart, also part of the team, about the relationship that he had with the team in India:

> "We talked through the nature of the relationship aspects that we had and hadn't clarified".

One of the key points emerging from the conversations that Matthew had subsequently was that the team was used to speaking a technical, more academic accounting language, and that Matthew's interactions with them in a more generalist language were getting in the way. Matthew explained to us how surprising this was to him, and what a change it has meant for him, as to date he had been working in an organisational culture which banned any jargon, so that he had become thoroughly used to talking a generalist language. He carried on explaining:

> "At the next meeting, I put all the jargon back, all the technical terminology and the accounting standards, the specific technical references. You could hear during the course of the meeting how the nature of the questions changed, the level of confidence and consensus rose. It was fundamentally different".

Exploring the issue with us a bit more, Matthew came to the realisation that the reason he could not develop a lasting shared understanding with the team about what needed to be done was very probably linked to the fact that the team was unsure as to whether they could trust Matthew's expertise, as he was using a language with them that did not reassure them. They had needed to use technical language with him in order to reassure themselves that Matthew knew what he was doing, and also, very probably, to understand Matthew better.

The conclusion to which we came was that the only way Matthew could build trust with that team was through his use of technical language. We were all baffled: none of us had expected that the use of technical language could make such a difference and un-stick the team in the way it did. Also I was noticing for myself how my understanding of trust was implicitly shifting: here it was not about purely relational aspects; the critical first step was about establishing one's credibility by speaking the same language, saying 'I am one of you'. In retrospect actually I would even expand this further, and argue that even the use of technical language can be a way of relating with others to build rapport and relationships.

During the session with Matthew, we all reflected further together and we arrived at the following key learning points from his case:

> The challenge that Matthew had to overcome in terms of adapting to the language and expectations of the Indian team while he was working virtually with them made clear to us the level of versatility that he needed to demonstrate. At the end of the day, he would have to use the generalist language with his parent company in the UK as well as when working virtually with his team in the US, but twenty minutes later he would need to switch quickly to a different language and way of interacting for a virtual meeting with his Indian colleagues.

> As Barbara mentioned, leaders always have to be versatile in the way they speak and interact with employees, the Board, the shareholders; however, what became very clear to us was that the level of versatility in terms of speed of adaptation is much quicker in the virtual space. In other words, one of the key aspects of effective leadership that Binney et al (2005) mentioned regarding the traditional leadership paradigm, namely 'working with the context' becomes stretched exponentially in the virtual space: the versatility and aptitude to adapt quickly, sometimes within one hour, to different contexts virtually seems to me to be a very critical aspect.

I hope that this story of Matthew's also provides a lively and useful example of the dependence of power on trust in the virtual space: if Matthew had not managed really to understand what he needed to do to develop trust between himself and his team in India, he would not have had any power, since he would have failed to achieve the task that needed to be completed.

When power gets in the way of trust

In the previous example we have seen that power depends on the way one manages to develop trust in the virtual space. With this next example we will explore how another form of power might get in the way of trust and destroy it.

In the subsequent collaborative inquiry group session, Barbara talked about her challenge, which quickly proved to be about power. She described her sense of failure because she had reached a situation where she needed to use her position, CEO of the organisation, to make things happen with her team in India. She said:

"In terms of getting what I needed, it worked, but it felt like reverting to the use of power [...] I feel that the fact that I used my power has affected the nature of my relationship with the team in India".

"How do you know?" asked Matthew.

"They communicate less, they share less what is going on as a way to regain their power" answered Barbara.

Our work with Barbara continued, and we explored the difference between what Barbara herself called 'earned power', the power that one gains through one's interaction with people and one's behaviour, and 'received power' generally known as positional power. This exploration of the topic with Barbara stretched over several consecutive sessions. Then in the fourth session there came a real breakthrough, not only for Barbara but for the four of us. Barbara explained:

"What I have become increasingly aware of since I joined this process [our collaborative inquiry] is how much I need to hold my power lightly if I really want to work well in the virtual space in India and Africa and be an effective virtual leader. If I use my [positional] power I get the answers that people think I want to hear. This might help me in the short term, but then if I go there I realise that things are not necessarily what I was told they were. They reward you with what they think you want to hear. [...] I realise how important it is to give up quite a lot of the power you have been given by the structure [...] This has been really illuminating to me while I have been in this process".

Barbara went on to underline how much she believed that as a virtual leader one has to give up one's authority, so that it does not get in the way of what she called real relationships, real exploration and real partnerships.

At this stage I tried to link Barbara's learning with a discussion we had in the second session when we explored Silvia's struggle in establishing her power in the context of her international key account team, where she had no positional power because no clear reporting structure existed. In that session we discussed how much she needed to invest time and effort into the relationship-building in order to make things happen. With Barbara we were discovering that when there is a clear reporting structure in place (the Indian team was clearly reporting to her) this positional power might actually become powerlessness in the virtual space, because it gets amplified there, becoming much stronger. Barbara added:

"Indeed every time I have been seduced into trying to use my positional power, this was amplified and my relationship with the team was damaged".

"Hence you lose the trust of your team, don't you?" I asked.

"Indeed! And then you need to use even more of your hierarchical power! It is a double bind!" Barbara answered.

"On the other hand, if you don't use your hierarchical power, then you gain trust from your team and trust becomes the real power that you need".

We all agreed with this conclusion. I could feel a real sense of truth in terms of what we were finding out; it was our truth about what seemed to make powerful relationships in the virtual space. I also realised how much the boundaries between trust and power, as one might define them in the traditional working and leadership paradigm, were becoming blurred and how interdependent trust and power could be in the virtual space.

A further interesting insight for me and for Silvia came with her realisation of how her view of her own power had shifted through the process of our collaborative inquiry:

"At the time that was the only way for me [to get power] by having more info [knowing more than my team members]. This gave me the right to say 'I lead'. I now want to question that".

She went on to explain how her own sense of her power had shifted and how she now thought that it was more related to the overall responsibility for the process:

"My power might really be more about taking responsibility for the overall process and the results".

Based on my personal experience of leading virtually and also linked to the emerging outcomes of the MilkCo interviews, I agree with her that power in the virtual space is not necessarily about knowledge but is linked more to the way one interacts with others and leads the process. From Silvia's insight, linked with the previous reflection on power related to Barbara's issue, an interesting image of power in the virtual space emerges: it seems that real power comes from hard work in establishing strong and trustful relationships and from leading a process that brings results and for which the leader takes responsibility. I am left with the image of a virtual leader as a trust builder.

> Panteli (2005) also comes to the conclusion that the use of hierarchical power in the form of coercive power negatively affects the development of trust. In her comparison with what she calls 'high trust global virtual teams' and 'low trust virtual teams' she notices that the 'high trust' teams used a facilitator who would pay great attention to the power dynamics in the team and to building trust, as opposed to the 'low trust' teams who would not use any facilitator.

The further multiple facets of trust and power in the virtual space

Having illustrated how the categories of trust and power might be shifting and connecting with each other in the virtual space, I want now to share further views on trust and power in the virtual space by tapping into different inquiry strands.

Trust is often seen as the 'glue' of virtual teams and, unfortunately, there is still the widely held belief that teams need first to meet face-to-face to be able to develop trust. I disagree with that.

> Several authors underline how critical trust is for teams to succeed in the virtual space.
>
> Luhmann (1973) underlines the importance of trust (in traditional leadership) particularly in complex and uncertain situations. I would argue – and several interviewees mentioned this – that the MilkCo teams started their work on the basis of a very unclear and complex question of what they needed to deliver. Hence Luhmann's statement seems to be particularly relevant: for him, trust begins where knowledge ends. It provides a reliable basis, namely the reliance on each other's actions and behaviours and thus one predictable parameter, in a complex gathering of uncertainties, unknown parameters and threats to cognitive solutions. Often trust is described as the 'glue' of virtual teams, for example see O'Hara-Devereaux and Johansen (1994, p 243).
>
> Remdisch and Utsch (2006) recommend face-to-face meetings between team members of virtual teams to develop trust; no wonder; they only ask leaders for their point of view based on their experience anchored in the face-to-face paradigm, which I think is the inherent problem with interviews if they are not combined with experimentation and reflection while embracing new approaches.

My work so far with clients in the virtual space – in over 80% of the cases I never meet my clients face-to-face – regularly shows that at the start of our work people do not feel that they can trust each other if they have not previously met face-to-face. After we have run one or two sessions with them, they change their point of view. I will come back to this point later in this section.

The research into trust in virtual teams has evolved a lot over time. People such as Handy (1995) or Lipnack and Stamps (1997) clearly advocate, like Remdisch and Utsch (2006), the need for face-to-face interactions to enable a virtual team to perform well virtually thereafter.

Others, for example Kirkman et al (2002), question this conventional thinking about trust in the virtual space, and claim that face-to-face is not mandatory for a virtual team to perform well. Wilson et al (2006) compared the development of trust in 52 teams, some being dispersed teams and others face-to-face, over a three-week period; as a result they go against the dominant perspective and claim that trust in distributed teams develops in the same way as it does in co-located teams, only with the exception that it takes longer to develop because it requires more time for members of those teams to exchange social information.

Others such as Oshri et al (2008) actually go so far as to claim that face-to-face meetings can be counter-productive for globally dispersed teams, as they are very time bound, can seldom be attended by all members of the virtual team in question, and cannot provide the long-term support required for the members' socialisation (Oshri et al base their view also on Furst et al, 2004).

Personally, I strongly agree with Oshri et al (2004): I have often observed that team leaders holding the belief (or having been told) that face-to-face is necessary to develop trust in their team take a pragmatic approach consisting in getting together face-to-face the people who can come together rather easily, and linking in others virtually (the more remote ones who would need too long to travel). In my view and experience this is the worst, most counter-productive combination to develop trust: the mix of face-to-face and virtual connection generates a gap between the ones face-to-face and the ones connected virtually, due to a distorted communication through a lack of 'equality' in the channels (see more detailed explanation in Invitation 1 'Virtual leaders need to learn, relearn and unlearn'). I have been called in to help virtual teams on many occasions where the main reason for the lack of trust in the team was precisely linked to this practice.

Trust for MilkCo's leaders

The MilkCo interviewees' views on trust in their virtual teams would certainly support Kirkman's views, and show that face-to-face is not necessary. At least seven people were very clear about what constituted trust in their teams:

"Trust is when people know what they are doing. I don't need to know the people involved in the process. For example I didn't know M before. M did a lot of preparation work. I was impressed by him and he gained my trust".

"Trust was there among almost all the people – apart from Z – he didn't give us his time. We didn't confront him because we had sympathy for his struggle. Trust existed among all others. I felt that they really wanted us to make progress".

"We were all excited about the subject. Everybody got involved and contributed. This is key for trust. If I had seen somebody not contributing, I would have lost my trust [...] Indeed knowing each other before is less important. The other ingredients such as contributing, listening well are much more important".

"I didn't know K before. Nevertheless I trusted him. He was competent, a good professional MD. You develop trust with one person or you don't. I did trust K even if I didn't know him".

"Trust is about knowing each other's capability, delivering what we promised. Trust was growing as a result. Also working together increased the trust level. Respect also increased. All were on time. Nobody let the others down".

"Trust is about being there when the meeting starts. It is a simple thing but a key one".

"I trust people who have concern for the quality of the work produced in the group, people who have concern about the active participation of all. I tend to discredit people with their own agenda. When I felt that people had worked, had prepared well, were eager to contribute, then I was more prone to trust them".

However, three interviewees still claimed that face-to-face was important for trust to develop. In two cases the interviewees presented it as a sine qua non; in the third case the interviewee felt that a face-to-face meeting up front did help the trust to develop.

I also had an interesting conversation with a further interviewee. When I asked him about trust he answered that there was trust in their team because they knew each other beforehand. He underlined the importance of the face-to-face prior to virtual working for trust to develop. Subsequently he happened to tell me the story of a woman with whom he had been working virtually for a while without having met her face-to-face. He then told me that he trusted her a lot. When I asked him why, he answered:

"She was summarising what she heard and checked for any misunderstanding. I felt listened to. I could sign off with no problems about what we had discussed and decided".

My interviewee then paused and noted how his views on trust had been changing in the course of our conversation:

"Now I have another answer!"

I am keen to mention this story because this pattern of reflection and thinking about trust in the virtual space corresponds to a lot of other experiences arising from my conversations with leaders and managers in different contexts. It seems to me that there is still a deeply embedded view that face-to-face is absolutely necessary to build trust in virtual teams. However when leaders start experiencing virtual working and are prepared to reflect on it, their view changes rapidly. There seems to be a parallel with the literature about trust in the virtual space, the development of which I mentioned earlier.

Three further interviewees were in full agreement with the notion of reliability and credibility, as well as the notion of wanting the whole team to succeed without pushing individual agendas through; however, they added a more subtle aspect regarding trust in the virtual space:

"Trust is a stomach feeling. It is about the way people answer. It is about intuition. You feel it. You don't need to have the body language to feel it. It is about the contents of the answers, the way people get involved. I can feel it over the phone".

"I have no need to see the person. I can lead people without seeing them. It is a personal thing, not a cultural one". [I had asked Q whether it was a cultural thing as he was Indian.]

Z told the story of a person he was working with at the moment [outside the 'virtual strategy process']:

"His world tells him not to trust me and vice versa. However we have found a good way to trust each other. I like to listen to the energy level in people's voices. If this fits with what they say, with their choice of words, and if their voice is clear, then I trust them. If there is a mismatch then I tend to distrust them".

At this stage I should mention that Z is maybe the most experienced one in the MilkCo group when it comes to working and leading virtually: he has done this for several years with people ranging from South America to the United States and Europe.

I am very impressed by the subtlety of the reflection of the last interviewee, and I can relate very strongly to his views and experience of trust in the virtual space. His views underline the importance of listening in a specific way (see Invitation 2). I also want to uphold the notion of trusting your intuition when you work virtually, as mentioned by one interviewee. In my own experience the more I work with the awareness of my body, the clearer I become about my 'gut' feeling, and I have been learning to use this 'data' with good results. This is confirmed by Charles Caldwell (2004) who speaks of the 'Virtual Management Intuition'.

Trust in the collaborative inquiry group with Barbara, Matthew and Silvia

Throughout our work together in the collaborative inquiry group, I had been journaling and taking personal notes about how I experienced us as a group. Building on my previous experience of the importance of developing good relationships in a virtual team before doing anything else, we had spent most of the first session talking about ourselves, and our interest and motivations for joining the group. I had personally paid careful attention to explaining to the group how I knew each member, and my story with each of them, particularly because I was the one bringing all four together (as mentioned none of them had actually met face-to-face).

We then went on to explore our research question and agree how we would work together. By the time we had finalised this, the session was over. Silvia was disappointed because she had wanted to 'start work', meaning the exploration of our question. However the development of our group proved that this investment in the relationship and setting the stage in the first session was time very well spent.

After the first session I was positively and recurrently surprised about how quickly the group came together. Although I was feeling reconfirmed in my hunch – also based on my experience of working with previous groups virtually – that trust can develop fast without people first meeting face-to-face, I was still surprised about that: it was as if I needed to surprise myself several times in a row finally to believe it! In my journal there are several sentences like:

> *"We speak together for ten minutes and already the group feels so intimate and trustful".*

I noticed this at every session. At regular intervals I invited the group to reflect on how we were working and feeling together, and I also shared what I noticed, wanting to cross-check this with my co-researchers.

The trust we were noticing could be described with several labels:

Low risk environment
Matthew explained that there was a lot of trust amongst us because it was

> *"a very low risk environment, a very appetising environment for me".*

Silvia agreed with this and added:

> *"You are in a neutral environment. You don't have to look strong. You are not being judged".*

I trust my friend's friends
Silvia also added something that I found really helpful:

> *"I trusted you [Ghislaine] and I know that you trust the others so I trusted them as well until they prove un-trustful. For me it was right from the start. I have never experienced that before".*

This statement is particularly interesting if one remembers that Silvia and I have never met face-to-face.

Common interests and self-interest
Several times the group underlined the commonality of their/our interest as being a strong driver for trust among us. In the last session Barbara said:

> *"I realised how different our respective contexts were and yet how strongly connected we all felt about virtual leadership despite these differences".*

Silvia expressed how happy she felt to have finally found somebody in Barbara who understood her issues around building relationships in the virtual space, and how well connected she felt with her.

I noticed that Barbara in particular was underlining specifically the importance of the fact that each of us had our own personal interest in being part of the group, and how this impacted on trust in the group. She then reached, in my view, an absolutely critical realisation:

"When I work with my virtual team how much do I take the time to understand the nature of our common interest as a team in spite of the time pressure? It is about TAKING [she was really emphasising this] the time to understand the nature of each individual's interest given their different contexts".

Actually I think that this is what we did in our collaborative inquiry group at the beginning: at the expense of Silvia feeling disappointed and impatient at the end of the first session because we had, in her view, not done any 'work'. We did take the time and great care to share our personal interests, and agree on our research question and how we would contribute to it, in the form of a robust psychological contract.

Deep in myself I felt very grateful to Barbara because she had managed to express a real need in leading virtually that I was sensing all the time but could not articulate for myself. In our last session, in an effort to consolidate our findings she further summarised that point as follows:

"I wonder whether there is a real need to be aware of other people's perspective, of what brings them in there and keeps them in there. It is about the need for the virtual leader to understand their self-interest".

Resonance

As well as, and in direct relation to the trust among us, I particularly noticed the resonance between us. By 'resonance' I mean here the web of strong and unconscious connection between the four of us, as for example Foulkes (1975) would describe in his concept of 'matrix'. As in many of the virtual action learning sets that I have facilitated, here the dance of thinking and feeling together was very strong, and was generating new thinking with a strong feeling of closeness where the sum of our thoughts and feelings was far superior to the four of us together. Barbara echoed this feeling and explained during the second session:

"I strangely feel very connected to you as a team. [although] we have only a loosely connected experience [of leading virtually]".

Trust for the 'Digital Natives'

I would like to finish this exploration of the topic of trust in the virtual environment by sharing some results of my research with the 'Digital Natives' leading to the same patterns of belief that prior face-to-face contact is necessary for trust to develop virtually. As mentioned, most of the leaders with little or no experience of leading virtually believe that face-to-face is needed. This seems to be a deeply embedded pattern that only practice and reflexivity (see glossary) can dispel.

In spite of the fact that all my young interviewees spend a substantial amount of time communicating virtually, all of them believe that you need to meet the person face-to-face if you are to trust them. They believe that seeing the person will enable them to judge whether the person is trustworthy or not, because of the eye contact and body language. The really important aspect however is that they also all feel that it is possible to develop a level of trust virtually, without having met the person, that is sufficient to do good work with him or her virtually. Thus the criterion of face-to-face-based trust applies only for their private relationships, and they all establish a clear divide between what they need for their private and for their professional relationships in terms of trust. This in my view raises several questions:

- Do they establish this divide because their experience of professional relationships is limited at this stage and they cannot really judge this aspect, or know what is 'good enough' trust?

> Having said this, the research on trust in the virtual space also conveys the concept of 'swift trust', which has some similarity. The concept of 'swift trust' was developed by Meyerson et al (1996) and relates to temporary teams (not necessarily virtual) who come together to achieve a specific task and disband after that. It describes the kind of trust necessary for team members to work well together: namely upfront trust, or suspending doubt, and a positive attitude. Meyerson et al (1996), as well as Jarvenpaa and Leidner (1998) who built on this concept for their work on virtual teams, underline the high degree of fragility and ephemerality of 'swift trust'.

- Do 'Digital Natives' have a conception of work that is maybe more transactional than that of people between 40 and 60 years old? If this is the case, what will be the impact of this new expectation on virtual working relationships?

- Assuming (and hoping!) that transactional working relationships will not be seen as sufficient in the future, at least for achieving, for example strategic or innovative work or to foster learning in virtual organisations, does this mean that virtual leaders will need to make even more effort and be more skilled than now to build and nurture trustful relationships virtually? The 'Digital Natives' might have a much more open attitude towards virtual working but a more 'functional' attitude towards working relationships.

Trusting upfront

I have learnt through years of practice that another aspect of trust in the virtual space is 'for a leader to be trusted it is important to trust others upfront'. For all the successful virtual leaders I have worked with the adage is: 'Trust until you are proven wrong' *rather than* 'distrust until they prove to you that they deserve your trust'.

I apply this principle myself and realise how helpful it is. The reason for this is a simple one. If I distrust people in the virtual space, people will feel it in a considerable way because, as explored earlier, the virtual space significantly amplifies any tension or emotion. If I trust people, they will feel it and the probability is high that they will trust me in return.

I am aware that the principle of trusting upfront might be challenging for some leaders who, because of their education and/or culture, might have learnt to be careful and not to trust people until they are completely sure. For example there is the much used maxim in German: 'Vertrauen ist gut, Kontrolle ist besser!' ('Trust is a good thing, checking things out is better!')

Moreover, asking leaders to trust others in the virtual space, a space where they might not feel completely comfortable to start with, might feel even more challenging. I can only encourage you at this stage to make the leap and to apply the principle. You will feel the difference.

Multi-faceted power for MilkCo leaders

The MilkCo interviewees found it more difficult to answer the question about power in their virtual teams than the one about trust. The ones who managed to describe their personal experience of power in their virtual teams had two main types of reaction.

For three of them power was about knowledge, expertise and information. M said: 'It is about showing that you know what you are talking about, then power is growing'.

However, the sponsor of the 'virtual strategy process' would refute the theory of virtual power through knowledge:

"I felt power a lot. I was owning it. They were putting lots of questions to me. It was about guiding people, giving directions, answering questions. It's not about knowing. It's enough to guide. It is a journey".

For others at MilkCo (a bigger group of eight people) power was more about how people relate and interact with others. This could take several forms and shapes. For example M explained:

"Power is not about information or expertise. It is about reiterating, reinforcing, coming back to it if you feel it is important. It is about using your voice, your words in a different way. You need to be convinced yourself and then you need to be versatile and know when to bring which arguments and with what timing".

For R power was

"about listening and really understanding what the person meant. It is also about listening well to be able to bring up your point in a clear way at the right time".

For S, power

"is about creating a common objective of wanting to achieve something together. Then you have power – you enthuse them".

For CH,

"Power also comes from the capability to offer structure to others".

According to MA:

"Power is when one contributes in a good way, eg when S presented slides, which were very helpful. She had done something and presented it. It doesn't come only from speaking. Also when you take notes and share your notes, you influence. It is HOW you contribute, not about your expertise".

For J,

"Power comes from getting feedback on what you are doing, whether you achieve results as a team. It comes also from giving support and enabling others. The expertise might give you the nomination. The power comes through the former aspects".

Finally there was one more specific view on power, from F:

"Power is about mastering the English language. It is about saying more with less. It is about your voice and how you work with it".

All the quotes and examples shown above seem to be acting as an echo of what came out of the collaborative inquiry group, and to illustrate that the power felt in the virtual space is an enabling power, a 'deserved' power as opposed to a 'given' power generated through one's position, status, etc. Indeed one of the most striking aspects was the role of hierarchical power in the virtual space. Most interviewees were very clear that as soon as a person was clearly representing hierarchy and making use of their hierarchical power, trust would be destroyed. People would become more careful and engage less, they would also become more silent. W summarised this as follows:

> "There is something more egalitarian [in the virtual space] than in face-to-face. Hierarchy does not play a role. However if you play on hierarchy from the start, then it can be devastating".

I would like to conclude this section simply by underlining the multiple facets of power in the virtual space: for some it is knowledge or expertise, for others it is about helping the team move forward, for others it is about really good listening, etc. Do these multiple facets reveal the complexity of power in the virtual space and/or a shifting concept that might actually be difficult to encapsulate in the language of power?

Power and control through technology: 'He who gets the buttons wins!'

To finish the exploration of the topic of power in the virtual space, let us consider how technology might be seen as giving an illusion of control, and therefore power, to the people leading the conversation.

When preparing for the virtual workshop with my Doctoral peers, my colleague and I carefully considered what I felt, based on my experience of virtual working with clients so far, were important choices to make. What are the types of 'privilege' that we ought to give to the participants: Should they be able to chat privately with each other? Should they be able to use the whiteboards at any time, etc.? It is worth noting that the terminology 'privilege' is precisely the one used by the WebEx platform. Other platforms use similar terminology.

When I work with clients I also pay careful attention to the choices I make, knowing that what the participants can do in the background of the formal process of interaction in the group will have a strong impact on the group, the experience and their engagement in the process. In the case of the Doctoral workshop my intention was to create an opportunity for all possible processes of interaction to emerge. I was keen to explore with my peers how we could all engage differently at the same time, and how we would make sense together and develop (or not) a sense of connectedness among ourselves in an environment so different from the one to which we were used.

At this stage I want to reflect further about the 'privileges' that my colleague Robert and I decided to assign to everybody in the group. In themselves the words 'privileges' and 'assign' have a strong power connotation. I am completely aware of the power that a facilitator and/or a virtual leader has when s/he hosts a session, just through the technology: you can give the power of expression and action to everybody (for example, they can open up a virtual whiteboard, write on it and share this with others while the facilitator explains something else using a set of slides that s/he presents in the same space) but you can equally take it away. After the workshop Mary, one of the participants, sent me some feedback by email and, regarding the topic of power, she immediately linked it with the technology and wrote:

> *"Power is an interesting question...because you opened up the tool set, we could all 'mess with' the content, which meant that you were sharing power. Typically, I am in sessions where someone is driving the information and my participation is always a function of the 'permission' they provide. [...] He who gets the most buttons wins! [...] You were much more open about sharing, so there was a shared sense of power for me. There were also lots of ways to get your attention, i.e., I could press a button or send you a note, so if I felt the need to have my voice heard, I was confident it would happen and I wouldn't be pushed off to the side or ignored".*

I remember clearly how irritated I became on one occasion, when we tested another virtual platform for InterCo, because they were keen that we use their platform for the virtual workshop that we were planning to run with their leaders. My colleagues and I quickly identified some structures that we felt were going completely against our own understanding of dialogue and real connectivity in the virtual space. For example, when a person wanted to speak they needed to raise their hand by clicking on a symbol and the facilitator would give them the microphone so that they could say what they wanted to say.

My colleague and I had to work really hard to help the client understand the importance of something they were perceiving as a detail. Changing the nature of virtual conversations to help them evolve into a more dialogic exchange and/or inquiry also means making conscious choices about the platform that one uses. This might still sound relatively straight forward. In my experience it is actually quite tricky, because in most organisations the choice of the virtual platform is made by the IT department, and the so-called 'users', the managers and/or leaders, have to live with this choice. Hence the technology chosen shapes the nature of the virtual interaction between the participants.

Furthermore the situation often becomes even trickier in my experience. In the cases of two of my clients, particularly with InterCo, the whole discussion ended up being a political one because IT was feeling questioned in their expertise since we, as external consultants dealing with the so-called 'soft' topics, were perceived as questioning the expert choice that they had made regarding the virtual platform. In the case of another client organisation, TopCo, the client ended up changing their platform after our intervention with them. We are not completely clear yet whether our intervention was the reason for the change of platform or whether it was just a coincidence. What we do know is that after our virtual workshop several participants became quite vocal about the poor choice their company had made in terms of virtual platform.

Finally I want to refer to Invitation 3, where I explained that one cannot control people's attention either in the virtual space or in the face-to-face. So while the temptation for leaders and providers of technology for virtual communication might be to offer even more features, (to control what a team member might be viewing while one is explaining and showing a concept in the virtual space) my strong advice is to resist the temptation to control, and to concentrate instead on winning people's attention by stimulating their senses as much, and in as diverse ways, as possible. I also reiterate the need for a leader to concentrate on 'share of ear' as opposed to 'share of voice' by offering compelling questions and provocations on which to work, so that all members are engaged.

So what?

You do not need to meet people face-to-face to trust them.

Resist the illusion of control and power offered by technology

The more you use your positional power, the less people will trust you in the virtual space

Instead ....

The more efforts you make to connect with your team members virtually, the more they will trust you. This means:

- Understand what really motivates them

- Understand what they really need

- Understand your team members' expectations in terms of language

Trust others until they prove you wrong

Reflect regularly on the following questions:

- When do I feel most trusted in the virtual space?

- When do I feel most trusting in the virtual space? What do I need to feel trustful?

- When do I feel most powerful in the virtual space?

- What are my real sources of powers in that space and how well do I use them?

Keep reflecting and learning ... don't look for an easy answer!

INVITATION 7
Shape Your Virtual Culture

In this invitation I claim that the current use of communication technology is mainly a mirror of the common practices and rules of communication. Users, virtual workers and virtual leaders cannot blame the technology for distorted communication. Instead they need to become aware of the choices they have, of the opportunities to shape the use of technology and hence the culture that they want to promote in their virtual teams. While they do not need to be technology experts, they do need to understand how to shape a culture using the technology in question through constant and careful choices, instead of letting themselves be shaped by it.

During the Doctoral workshop one peer, Denis, mentioned:

"We are exploring using it [the virtual platform WebEx] in a way that doesn't reflect the way it was designed".

Indeed the platform we had chosen seems to have been designed within a 'tell' or 'command and control' paradigm, rather than an inquiry paradigm where all can co-create and develop ideas independently of power differentials - see Invitation 3 ('Don't Control, Connect') and Invitation 6 ('Your Power is Trust'). During our thorough research at Ashridge we found that WebEx was one of the platforms coming closest to our aspirations.

Technology is to serve you, not vice versa!
In the virtual space, it requires some thinking through and planning to enable a team to work in an inquiry way, where all voices have the same value and status instead of letting the work happen in a way in which the official leader 'chairs' the session and tells others what to do. For me this raises an intriguing question: If the technology currently is a mirror of common practice in virtual working, what will it take to make it evolve? Should the practice evolve and define itself first and then the technology will follow, or vice-versa, or should both happen at the same time? Certainly I feel that the last will be the case. I have actually started some conversations with technology

experts, to see how we could work together to evolve this paradigm in the virtual environment, because I am convinced that there is much to be learnt, in terms of what might become possible, from researchers and developers of communication technologies.

> I would like to underpin my statements with the views of Woolgar (1991a and 1991b) who explains that technology cannot be thought of independently of the users:
>
> *"[...] the machine becomes its relationship to the user, and vice versa"* (1991a, p.89) and
>
> *"This suggests that characteristics of society play an important part in deciding which technologies are adopted. Hence technology cannot be construed as a factor 'independent' of society. Second, the same technology can have different effects in different situations"* (1991 b, p. 30).
>
> In their research on technology appropriation by young people, Carroll et al (2001) also confirm this view of technology as socially constructed.

My experience of working with 'Digital Natives' shows that, on the one hand, the latter do not have any inhibition regarding the use of technology to communicate, and they also seem to be more versatile than older generations when it comes to choosing which technology to use for what purpose. The European youngsters I worked with would use Facebook a lot, as opposed to the America-based ones who would prefer to use MSN (originally 'Microsoft Network', now more frequently called Windows Life Messenger and Windows Life Groups). The reason for this difference is linked to the quality of the connection which, according to my interviewees, varies a lot depending on where one is based. All of them would use Facebook or MSN for several purposes such as: keeping their friends informed about what they are doing and remaining connected with them (e.g. Marion and Pamela would keep their friends updated about their activities such as travelling by posting pictures on a regular basis), inviting their friends to a party, looking at the profiles of their peers-to-be and deciding who they might want to start to contact before meeting them face-to-face at university.

I was also struck by the clarity of views of my Brazilian interviewees on the use of Skype (camera and phone line, i.e. audio and video modes combined). Erika explained that she would only use Skype (audio and video combined) with intimate friends as opposed to acquaintances. She gave me two reasons for this: firstly, because the picture on Skype is not always clear so you must know the person well in order not to be distracted by the poor picture quality. Secondly, the combination of picture and audio in the virtual world equates for her (her friends in the interview also agreed with her) to more intimacy. For acquaintances, she would prefer to use MSN to maintain more distance by using a word-only based communication platform.

Nevertheless, in all my interviews the cost aspect is the overriding factor, particularly for youngsters. So, for example, Marion would be very clear on the cost of SMS compared with Facebook, MSN or Skype. All the interviewees were also very clear on when to use which medium, for what purpose and at what cost; e.g. SMS would be mostly used for urgent matters, whereas organising a party would happen on Facebook, unless you run like Maya – a free competition of 5,300 SMS a month and try to win it by beating the record!

My experience with leaders in organisations is that they are often more inhibited by the use of technology to communicate and, most importantly, once they learnt one or two technologies and felt more comfortable with them, they tended to stick with them for their virtual work throughout, rather than asking themselves: is this the right technology and medium for what I want to achieve with my team?

For example, when a leader gets used to and starts to like blogging s/he often tends to want to use blogs for many virtual activities with his/her team, and does not always question whether blogging is the most sensible thing to do, given the particular goal that s/he has in mind. I have come across many leaders who are disappointed when, having launched a blog on a specific topic, and after the first phase of excitement in the team and/or organisation, the traffic slows down and the whole initiative fizzles out. Unless the purpose, even more critically the process and the responsibilities for facilitating and containing the blogging activities are clarified, in my experience blogs (at least the ones in organisations) are condemned to fail. I am always amazed to observe how leaders start a blog and expect it to flourish on its own, and be self-sustaining.

Another example is when people use a videoconferencing system simply because this is what they feel most comfortable with, but without checking whether this is the most appropriate technology to use for what they want to achieve. In addition to the points mentioned in Invitation 2 ('Listen, Forget Body Language!') I would argue that using a videoconference to update each other on the progress made in a project is not the best use of people's time. Firstly, people might end up spending more time sorting out technological difficulties than actually connecting personally and working. Secondly, because of the time lost with technical difficulties at the start, they tend to skip the personal connecting phase in their meeting and dive directly into the task, in their view, to maximise the use of the remaining time. This becomes a vicious circle: technological problems get in the way and reinforce the view of participants that working virtually is difficult. Less time is available for the meeting, and the first thing which gets skipped to make up for lost time is that time scheduled to enable people to connect at a personal level (to use some facilitation jargon: the 'check-in' moment) – if any time had been planned for this at all – so that people go straight into the task. This, in turn, reinforces people's view that virtual working will only be second-class.

Sticking a little longer with the same scenario, I want to underline a further challenge that I often recognise when coaching virtual teams. When I work with a team whose members are spread across the world and, due to incompatible time zones, have the video conference at a time when some people have to get up at 4.00 am and others need to stay awake until midnight, I want to make sure that when I have them all together I make best possible use of this synchronous (see glossary) time. This means using the asynchronous (see glossary) time to inform people about the current status of the work (and asking them to read everything before the meeting) so that when they come together the synchronous time can be used for questions, discussions, decision making, reflection, etc. In other words the virtual leader is best served when considering the mix of technologies and media for each specific purpose. For example, what can be done asynchronously – before the meeting – and communicated via email or on the company's shared site (e.g. Sharepoint); what has to be done when all are together virtually and for this, is a teleconference, a video-conference or a web-based meeting (where all can work on the same document and are connected via the phone) the best technology? I would argue that, when it comes to meetings about decision making and/or developing new ideas, using a web-based meeting where people can co-create documents and speak spontaneously on the phone is by far the best available technology.

Dealing with conflicts virtually
One of the most critical skills for effective virtual leadership is for leaders and teams to know how to handle conflicts virtually. The first hurdle to overcome is to avoid waiting to deal with the conflict until the next face-to-face meeting with the team (which – if at all – might happen only next year), since the lingering issue will distort communication, damage trust and performance. Conflicts are an integral part of working relationships; they are

normal and represent significant opportunities for a team to grow – also in the virtual space!

The second challenge is to decide how best to handle the conflict virtually. Many readers will probably already have had a bad experience of conflicts which were escalated via email, with an endless email chain and an ever growing distribution list, resulting in loss of trust and complicated situations from which it is almost impossible to recover. The rule I offer, based on my experience, is to use a synchronous, voice-based means of communication (video is not necessary – see Invitation 2 'Listen, Forget the Body Language').

In other words, if you feel an underlying conflict, react to it sooner rather than later and pick-up the phone. If the person is not in the right place (either in terms of surroundings or in terms of mental place e.g. because of time pressure) at the moment you call, agree on the best time to speak and call again. If you feel that there is an underlying conflict between two or several people in your team, contact them on a one-to-one basis first and explore, then contract with them to have a teleconference with all and be mindful of how you choose the timing for the teleconference (see Tool Box D) and ask them to apply the virtual meeting hygiene principles (see Tool Box A).

In summary, to deal successfully with conflicts virtually, the one-on-one communication step followed by the collective communication step (where applicable) is critical as is the synchronous dimension (as opposed to the asynchronous mode like using emails). Based on my experience, in this context video communication is not necessary. On the contrary this might distract from in-depth connection at a personal level (see Invitation 2).

The Communication Designer

As explained through the above examples, I suggest that the virtual leader must be able to *design* communication in the same way as a fashion designer. While colours, textiles, shape and size are the key parameters for the latter, the former needs to think in the following dimensions:

- What needs to happen on a one-on-one basis as opposed to on a group basis?

- What needs to happen synchronously as opposed to asynchronously?

- What needs to happen with audio only or audio & web-based (e.g. Live Meeting, WebEx, etc) or audio & web-based with cameras or audio & video based (e.g. Telepresence or Tandberg)

Knowing how to work in these dimensions and to combine them is one of the key competencies of a virtual leader. Does it mean that a virtual leader needs to be a technology expert? Not at all! It means, however, first and foremost that to be successful the virtual leader needs to ask him/herself what s/he wants to achieve, with whom and what is the best way to communicate. It might also mean, as a result, that the virtual leader has to seek the help of a communication technology expert regarding a technology that s/he does not yet know.

The diagram below shows the key parameters for the virtual leader's choice.

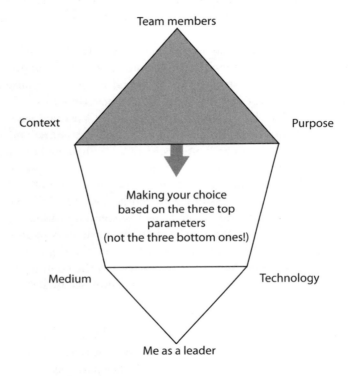

Figure 4: The virtual communication diamond

I often observe that leaders choose the telecommunication platform based on the lower parameters, i.e. according to what they know (me as a leader: what do I know, feel most comfortable with), the technology readily available that they use most of the time and transfer the communication medium they use face-to-face (e.g. a PowerPoint presentation) on to the virtual space without taking into consideration the idiosyncrasies of that space.

In my experience, successful virtual leaders need to proceed in the opposite direction: they should ask themselves what is the profile of my team members (how technology-literate are they?), what do I want to achieve in this meeting? (e.g. only share information and comment, or take important decisions, or generate new ideas?) and what is the situation for my team members (e.g. will they be travelling at the time we have the meeting, and will it be difficult for them to find a stable internet connection?). The choice of the telecommunication platform and the medium to use should be based on the *top three parameters*.

Ideally, leaders should discuss this 'communication diamond' in their virtual team when they begin to work together as a virtual team (it is never too late to do this if you have not done it so far though!) and decide with all members about when to communicate, in which way, using which platform, and what to expect from everyone involved. So doing, virtual leaders would have the best chance to shape and nurture the best culture in the virtual team, by making collective and conscious choices instead of going on automatic pilot mode and being led by the technology.

Some guidance is provided in the Tool Box regarding which communication platform is helpful for which purpose. The table (Tool Box E) can be used as a starting point for discussion with team members, based on their literacy in terms of technology and the ways of working that the team wants to adopt.

Finally, my point here is not about encouraging your company to buy more technology. Increasingly I discover that organisations are actually already pretty well-equipped in terms of technology. The difficulty is more that some technology, once purchased, does not get used or users become disillusioned because it does not bring the expected results. Technology is often made responsible for something it cannot deliver, namely human connectivity.

Watch the terminology: words make worlds!

I have always been intrigued by the terminology used by many providers in the virtual space. For example, as mentioned, it is common to come across words such as 'privileges' or 'war rooms'. With 'privileges', providers mean the features on the virtual platform, for example enabling the participants to make some comment on the virtual whiteboard or to use the chat room to exchange personal views with colleagues during the virtual meeting. Why should these features be called 'privileges'? What are the implications of this? If participants are assigned these privileges they can actually simply contribute in a free, spontaneous way, which is in my view what should be advocated to develop real dialogue in the virtual space. In my view these features are not 'privileges' they are 'essentials' i.e. basic necessary features for real connectivity in the virtual space.

On the contrary, in my view, 'privileges' implies that these can be taken away from the participants again – which is the way these features are conceived. If these 'privileges' are taken away from participants, this implies some sort of in-built technical power for the virtual leader (or chairperson or facilitator) and the meeting turns quickly into a virtual event where participants are asked or told what to do or when to answer, without inviting them to think and learn together.

I am also irritated by the term 'war room'. A virtual 'war room' is for example a specific site dedicated to a project team where the members can log-in and find the necessary information regarding their ongoing project (e.g. project plan, minutes of meetings, etc.) and the team members (e.g. list of team members with individual details such as time zone in which they work, email addresses, profile etc.). The actual expression 'war room' is not very conducive to – or at least not consistent with – the concepts of cooperation, collaboration, innovation, creative exchange, etc. so important in the virtual space. Why technology providers still keep this terminology remains a real mystery to me!

My personal experience has shown that technology suppliers are unfortunately usually not the most flexible when it comes to modifying the features and terminology of their product. This means that, as virtual leaders and/or facilitators, we need to be particularly mindful of how and when we use the terminology of the platform we choose to utilise.

To conclude, in a rather philosophical way, I would like to mention Hine (2000) who makes a very helpful analysis and establishes the contrast between two emerging views on the Internet. The first view of the Internet is that it represents a place, cyberspace, where culture is formed and reformed and constantly shaped and renegotiated, based on people's backgrounds, cultures, learning, etc.. The second view of the Internet is that it is a cultural artefact or a representation of how we think and behave in general. So far, in Hine's eyes, the second view has been privileged and I fully agree with her. My findings show that the first view deserves more focus and research.

The question of effective virtual leadership is at the core of the first view: we as leaders have a choice of how we shape our interactions on the Internet (or virtually) and we need actively to make that choice. This obliges us, however, to revisit in depth how we have shaped our identity and our relationships with others and our environment so far. The potential of entering into a new territory lies in this process of questioning the way we have been constructing our identity and relationships to others and the universe.

So what?

- Think first about **what you want to achieve** in the virtual space and **with whom** you want to do this: then make your choice accordingly in terms of technology and medium. **Design** your communication. (For some guidance on this, see Tool Box E)

- Get help where and when needed.

- Do not go into automatic pilot; do not use what you have always used; do not do what you have always done.

- Words make worlds: shape the culture of your team – **do not let technology providers shape it for you!**

- Apply some basic hygiene principles:

- Whatever technology you use, check it beforehand with each partici- pant. A test of 10 minutes with each team member a few days before the meeting will make a huge difference to the quality of the virtual meeting experience

- Ask people to join 10 minutes (or 5 depending on the complexity of the technology you use) before the official start of the meeting so that potential last minute technology problems (you will have them most of the time!) can be overcome in time for a prompt start of the meeting

- See Tool Box A and B for further virtual meeting hygiene principles.

INVITATION 8
WHO Are You?

In this section, I describe how leaders need to have the willingness, confidence and capability to be self-reflexive. This requires taking risks and challenging the status quo in terms of managing, as well as deeply questioning their identity as leaders. One change in behaviour that is most likely to be required is that of slowing down – a difficult change in our fast moving world, but one on which I focus here.

The examples that I describe below illustrate the difficulty that my co-inquirers have when it comes to reflecting on their leadership in the virtual space. The same applies to most of the leaders I work with in the context of my consulting activities. Initially, they do not perceive themselves as *leaders* in the virtual space. They focus more on management.

My first example comes from my work with InterCo. My colleague and I decided to conduct a series of preparatory interviews with the participants for the Virtual Leadership programme that we delivered. After the interviews I was most struck by the following:

- When we asked the participants to describe themselves as virtual leaders, they found it very difficult to answer. Either they said hardly anything, or they answered about themselves as leaders in general or they spoke about themselves as managing activities virtually (e.g. sending reports, commenting on results in a teleconference, informing others by phone). Some of them claimed to do up to 70% of their work in a virtual environment, but they would not consider their leadership in that virtual environment.

- When I asked them about the moments in the virtual environment when they felt at their best, they usually gave me examples about management activities, such as getting a performance report, convening a teleconference to share the financial data, etc.

- Why is it, I asked myself then, that the interviewees did not consider themselves as influencing and/or leading in the virtual space, although they clearly had the responsibility to lead a team, the members of which they saw approximately 4 or 5 times a year? I was puzzled by this. It was as if they automatically link the fact of leading (e.g. working on relationships, motivating or what they call the 'soft' aspects) with face-to-face meetings.

On another occasion, ten diverse, very senior clients who did not know each other joined me for a vivid conversation on virtual leadership. Most of the attendees explained that they had to lead virtual teams and that this was the reason why they joined the conversation. They seemed to struggle less with the concept of virtual leadership and my question about their personal virtual leadership. At the end of the meeting, five of them said that they had found the conversation very helpful and that it had been the first time that they had had the opportunity to speak about and explore their virtual leadership. So they were not questioning the legitimacy of the concept in itself, but they were acknowledging that this topic is not yet much addressed, and how good they felt about having had the opportunity to talk about it.

The first thing that struck me when working with my co-inquirers (William, Sten and Silvia) was that they had similar difficulties in reflecting on their leadership in the virtual space.

Firstly there was the sheer difficulty and newness for them of thinking through the theme of leading virtually, and therefore of talking about their virtual leadership. So far my co-inquirers felt that they had to manage tasks and information virtually; but they did not see themselves as leaders in the virtual space.

Secondly, one could argue that reflecting on one's leadership does not come naturally to leaders, whether they lead in the traditional way (by 'traditional way of leading' I mean a leadership that happens mostly face-to-face, but of course would include emails and phone calls) or virtually.

Ladkin (2010), in her book *Rethinking Leadership,* suggests that this has been one of the reasons why it is difficult to study leadership. She introduces the concept of 'ready-to-hand' engagement (when "the 'things' we use 'disappear' into the purposes for which they are being used") and explains that most of the time leaders don't stop to reflect on their leadership until something goes wrong and/or unless somebody invites them to reflect:

> "The fact that those involved in 'doing' leadership have difficulty articu-
> lating what they do does not mean leadership itself does not exist. The
> difficulty arises when attempting to move from a 'ready-to-hand' engage-
> ment with leadership, in which it is seamlessly enacted and thus not
> consciously available, to a 'present-at-hand' examination of it, whereby it
> 'freezes' for an instant and can be subjected to closer scrutiny" (Ladkin
> 2010, pp.45-46).

I think this phenomenon is well illustrated by Sten's reaction during our first session: He commented that virtual leadership had been an unknown topic for him until I mentioned it. He told me what his boss said when he informed him that he wanted to be part of my inquiry: 'Isn't it what you are trying to do? Isn't it what I am trying to do also?' Sten explained to me how, for both of them, 'the penny dropped' in that moment. When I asked him why he didn't realise this earlier, Sten's answer was:

"I don't think so much about it [...] I just do what needs to be done".

The virtual strategy process initiative at MilkCo turned out to be a great success overall, and all the people I have talked to have been extremely posi- tive about what they learnt and achieved. Nevertheless, most of them said that at the beginning of the process they were sceptical as to whether it would work, and especially whether they would be able to do the work to the quality required. It was a big surprise to them that it worked. One of my interviewees said:

"We actually worked together [...]. I was really impressed that we were able to achieve so much. I did not expect this at the beginning".

Another person said:

"At the end I thought, WOW, that was really a good process"

and added:

"What we did in four months we would not have been able to do in two years [if we had done this face-to-face]".

Several people shared that opinion. They also felt that people were much more focused on the work in the virtual space. A further participant said:

"We also had lots of fun virtually! That was a surprise. I thought that this was only possible face-to-face".

While all my interviewees were very clear and positive about the benefits of the process and what they had achieved, it was more difficult, at least for some of them, to reflect on the leadership aspects of their work in the virtual space. It took them some time during the interviews to enter into a reflexive mode and make sense of the critical moments in their virtual leadership. This confirmed to me again that, for many leaders, leading in the virtual space is either something that they might do automatically without taking the time to reflect on it, or more probably that it is something that they usually don't do at all, which is why they fail in their role as leaders of virtual teams.

The same happened with William, Sten and Silvia. When I started my work with them I quickly found that I had to let go of most of my questions, because these were far too sophisticated for them. My co-researchers were only starting to become aware of the topic and struggled to address specific questions. The typical questions which they would find difficult to answer would be for example: When did you feel at your best when leading in the virtual space last week? William, Sten and Silvia were not making a clear distinction between their face-to-face leadership and their virtual leadership; they sensed that there were different challenges related to their virtual leadership but struggled to identify their nature.

After some exploration, the three of them started noticing some difference. But each of them framed this difference between leading virtually and leading primarily in the traditional way ('traditional way' – see glossary) in a different way.

For William, at first the key challenge was how to establish a structure in the virtual world (as a source of reliability and stability). For Sten, it was more about how to be prepared and present in the moments of synchronous (see glossary) connection. For Silvia, it was the need to establish her credibility and legitimacy as a virtual leader through having more information and knowledge than the other team members.

At the beginning William and Sten thought personal contact had to happen face-to-face (combining 'personal contact' and 'virtual' was an oxymoron in their minds), and they were saving the personal conversations for the face-to-face meetings, instead of exploring ways of establishing and developing real personal contact in the virtual environment. Silvia had a different approach; she had had no opportunity to do other than establish personal contact with her team members virtually because the team rarely met face-to-face.

The first eight to nine months of my work with William and Sten were mostly characterised by what I would call 'an intellectual flirt' with the topic of virtual leadership. While I noticed their openness to discussing the topic and ways in which to practice, they would not really have a go and experiment with the ideas that they developed with me on the phone. However, when I decided to become more directive towards them, they finally went for it and experimented with different practices. William in particular then developed a wealth of practice that I could only follow with amazement. He had found his own place in the world of leading virtually, and was clearer about his identity and role as virtual leader, as after a while was Silvia. Sten's story is slightly different, as my work with him stopped after 12 months because he changed his role and leading virtually was not required to the same extent in his new job.

In retrospect I wonder whether the difficulty that my co-researchers were experiencing could be thought of as the difficulty of moving from reflection to reflexivity. Cunliffe (2009) clearly defines the difference between these. Reflection is understood to be a cognitive or intellectual activity, consisting of thinking about something in an objective, logical and neutral way, based on a realist view of the world with a reality to be discovered, measured, categorised and properly explained. Reflexivity, on the other hand, is based on a social constructionist view of the world; in other words there is not one single reality of the world – we shape our own social and organisational realities.

> "[...] reflexivity goes deeper than reflection, because it means interrogating the taken-for-granted by questioning our relationship with our social world and the ways in which we account for our experience". [...]
> "Being self reflexive means questioning our own ways of being, relating and acting" (Cunliffe 2009).

Let me illustrate this hypothesis in more detail, with some additional examples.

As mentioned, in the first phase of my work with them, William and Sten would engage intellectually with the topic, but would refrain from actually experimenting and thinking about themselves in this new context. They sensed that this would require them to question more radically both their practice and their own sense of identity.

Here I would like to illustrate the point that I have just made by sharing a story about something that happened with William. In the early stages of working with him, William showed me the internal webpage that he wanted to put in place so that his team members could read information about the division and the different plants. On this page he wanted to publish regular personal words to his team. He had also asked his assistant to place his picture on the website, but he commented to me that he did not like this picture. When I asked why, he said:

"Because I look tired, I don't look upbeat".

I answered:

"But William, you have just told me that you are exhausted. What is wrong in showing a picture of a tired William? Are people who currently meet you face-to-face not seeing that you are tired? Why do you think that it has to be different in the virtual space?"

(William very much defines himself as an authentic person.) He was quiet on the phone for what felt like a good while, and finally I checked with him:

"Does what I am trying to question make sense?"

He answered:

"Absolutely! It is just that I had never thought about it like that! I have been exhausted for several months now [his organisation was going through tremendous change and he was under a huge amount of pressure] and actually it would be the most unnatural thing to show a picture of me that looked full of energy with a smile all over my face!"

I waited a bit and let silence unfold, thinking through the implications of what William was saying and trying to follow his thinking. I then asked him:

"Have you ever thought about what type of leadership and what kind of picture of you as a leader you want to convey to your team in the virtual space?"

William had not thought about it but he was eager to start doing so. The following year was going to be a very intense one for him, questioning his own sense of identity and his virtual leadership.

When Sten and William finally decided to 'jump into the cold water' they had no choice but to open up for the more radical questioning of their taken-for-granted views of managing, and of themselves as managers and leaders. Later, when I asked William why he finally started acting and experimenting with different activities virtually, his words were unequivocal:

"You said to me that I had to try it out. I had to risk my image; potentially I might lose face. Now the conqueror in me is proud of myself because it has become part of me; I don't question it any longer; nobody does; it has become part of the normal things to do in our management team. But at that time, when you told me to use music [...] I thought: Can I do this? Am I a sissy? Will they see me as a 'shrink'? What I am doing is very controversial for a manufacturer. Some people think: Oh this is a typical William thing again!"

At this stage I ought to explain the use of music mentioned by William. He had been thinking hard how he could develop a feeling of togetherness virtually across the different plants in Europe that he led. He had previously had different ideas of using imagery, which he had implemented with some success, but he was still not completely satisfied. I shared with him my views about music and how one can use music in virtual meetings to help develop a common emotional field among people.

My original thinking had been very much influenced by Heron's concept of the 'Unified Affective Field' (1999) and I had developed ideas about how to use music to offer, up front, a kind of emotional field, a common ground where people across geographies would meet and connect with each other at a level other than the task.

In William's case, he was able to rethink his way of being with others and his way of leading only when he started experimenting with new ways of connecting with them.

Implications

During numerous conversations with consultants about my research, one very experienced German consultant, Martin, for whom I have a lot of respect, said to me:

> "Actually, leading virtually is nothing new when it comes to the WHAT, it is all about achieving the same things that every leader needs to achieve in the face-to-face too. Only the way of doing it is different. For example when you speak about communication, listening, trust, these are also things that one needs to attend to in face-to-face".

At that time I found it difficult to respond, but I felt intuitively that somehow this statement was not right. I can now better express my view of virtual leadership in relation to what Martin was claiming.

More than the WHAT or the HOW, the thing that really seems to matter is the question of WHO. As a virtual leader, I need radically to reconsider my own sense of myself and my sense of others, how I relate to them, how I relate to my environment and space and time. Attempting to lead effectively virtually cannot be done just by transferring into the virtual space what one has learnt to do well face-to-face.

Inevitably, leading effectively virtually leads me to reconsider these fundamental questions. It is as if the answers that I give to the WHO I am and how I am in this world come first and will have an impact on the WHAT I do and HOW I do it. One could argue that this is also valid in traditional leadership, but I believe that this type of questioning is particularly critical in the virtual space, otherwise the whole team construct and my leading of it might fall apart rapidly. It is as if leading virtually accelerates and amplifies a need that has been present for a long time.

The virtual leader needs to make conscious choices, based on an all-encompassing deepened awareness and grounding, in terms of physical/sensorial, intellectual/existential and spiritual noticing. These allow the exploration of new territories regarding our sense of existence as individuals, groups and organisations. Virtual working and virtual leading offers an excellent opportunity to explore our **being,** and to know ourselves better as human beings. Not only does it offer this opportunity; it makes it a sine qua non for good connectivity and effective leadership in the virtual space.

Paradoxically, it is not about pushing our awareness beyond our physical body; on the contrary it is primarily about knowing ourselves better in our embodied selves, and realising how, so far, our mind has led us to define the norms (Lakoff & Johnson 1999), the normal and the abnormal. It is more about being than thinking and doing. Furthermore, and as a consequence, I would argue that by becoming an effective virtual leader I become a more grounded leader, because I need to develop a sharper awareness, new skills and capabilities.

Hence, in my eyes, effective virtual leadership requires triple loop learning. I attempt to represent this in the model below.

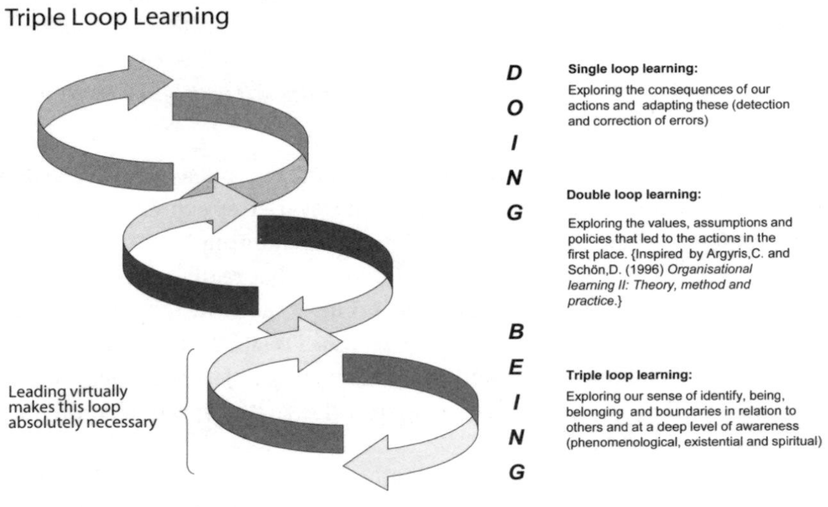

Triple Loop Learning

D O I N G

Single loop learning:
Exploring the consequences of our actions and adapting these (detection and correction of errors)

Double loop learning:

Exploring the values, assumptions and policies that led to the actions in the first place. {Inspired by Argyris,C. and Schön,D. (1996) *Organisational learning II: Theory, method and practice.*}

B E I N G

Triple loop learning:

Exploring our sense of identify, being, belonging and boundaries in relation to others and at a deep level of awareness (phenomenological, existential and spiritual)

Leading virtually makes this loop absolutely necessary

Figure 5: The triple loop learning model

I am aware that the concept of triple loop learning in itself is not new. In the last decade other researchers have developed very similar concepts unrelated to the virtual space. I reference here in particular the concept of triple loop awareness, coined by Starr and Torbert (2005), or of triple-loop learning described by Peschl (2007). Although I developed the above concept unaware of the existence of the former two, I am very much struck by the degree of similarity between all three.

The concept presented by Starr et al (2005) of a triple loop awareness focuses on the notion of awareness and presence:

"Contrasting it with single- and double-loop feedback in a person's awareness, the triple loop supposedly affords the capacity to be fully present and exercise re-visioning, frame-changing, timely leadership" (Starr et al 2005, p.85).

It is not about specific actions, or even overall strategies that leaders can develop, but more about our very present awareness, so that we feel our own presence and that of everything and everybody around us. According to Starr et al this kind of awareness then enables the individual to transcend their habitual patterns of understanding, and recognise how these are guiding and limiting their understanding. In other words, this awareness is also of a trans-conceptual nature; for example it enables us to transcend the concept of time or 'here and now' (which I explore in Invitation 3).

For Peschl (2007), triple-loop learning concerns the existential level. It is mainly about redirecting one's attention from the outside world into one's interior world and, through an acute awareness, noticing what is emerging from within. It is not about 'looking for something' but about 'letting something come to you', the latter being something deeply connected with your will, deep intention and purpose. Peschl explains that the moment of 'letting something come to you' might feel like a moment of emptiness that can cause existential fear in some cases, because one loses the knowledge-based ground on which one stands, which normally provides a cognitive framework (Peschl 2007).

Both aspects, the one of being fully present as a way to transcend given concepts, and the one of directing one's attention towards the inside as opposed to looking for the answer out there, constitute key parts of Otto Scharmer's (2007) so-called Theory U, or the second type of learning model, which I would like to represent as follows:

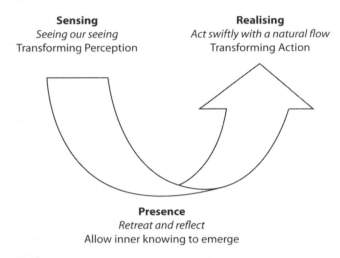

Sensing
Seeing our seeing
Transforming Perception

Realising
Act swiftly with a natural flow
Transforming Action

Presence
Retreat and reflect
Allow inner knowing to emerge

Figure 6: The Theory U by C. Otto Scharmer (2007)
Adapted version

The first element of 'sensing' in the model of Scharmer, to my mind, is key, because it involves the need to slow down in order to see with fresh eyes – to become aware and to stop habitual ways of thinking and perceiving.

Senge, Scharmer et al (2005, first published in 2004) mention an interview with Master Nan Huai Chin, regarded in China as the most important living Buddhist master, and a major force in the revival of Buddhism in that country. Master Nan Huai Chin is also considered by some to be 'the' eminent Confucian scholar:

"Master Nan then added that the core of the Confucian theory of leadership formation rests on the idea that 'if you want to be a leader, you have to be a real human being'. You must recognize the true meaning of life before you can become a great leader. You must understand yourself first". (Senge, Scharmer, et al 2005)

The authors underline that the

"success of an intervention depends on the inner condition of the intervener" and

"that's far more important than techniques or strategies for change".

They demonstrate that the leadership required in our global institutional networks and organisations paradoxically comes back to the old idea of the 'cultivated self' as the 'leader's greatest tool' to cultivate the wisdom of groups and larger social systems:

"That's why I think that cultivation, 'becoming a real human being', really is the primary leadership issue of our time, but on a scale never required before. It's a very old idea that may actually hold the key to a new age of 'global democracy'".

For me Senge and Scharmer's words echo Wilber's view on leadership:

"Simply focusing on the global technological net misses a truly crucial feature: what levels of consciousness are moving through that net? What good is it if the entire globe is at moral stage I? That would merely spell global war. [...] - unless we put as much attention on the development of consciousness as on the development of material technology - we will simply extend the reach of our collective insanity. This was also the conclusion reached by UNICEF [...], namely, that without interior development, healthy exterior development cannot be sustained". (Wilber 2001)

Wilber's (2001) words 'without interior development, healthy exterior development cannot be sustained' resonate very strongly with my findings. As I mentioned, exploring the question of 'who I am' is most critical, and experimenting with this new understanding is required if one wants to lead virtually. One could call this 'self-cultivation' in Senge et al's terms. In so doing I become a 'real human being' (in Master Nan's terms), hence I become 'a real leader'. Interestingly, if cultivating self is the most critical condition to leading effectively virtually, then by learning to lead virtually I become a ***real*** leader.

All the different perspectives that I have shared above seem to point to the need for higher levels of awareness being necessary to inform deeper levels of knowing and decision making. Only when I manage to work with the question of WHO I am as a virtual leader will I be able to be effective, and overcome the challenges encountered by most leaders in the virtual space.

The hypothesis is that the reason why leading and working virtually have for most so far remained a challenging and unsatisfactory experience is precisely because leaders, researchers and management theorists have concentrated on the How and the What but have neglected the Who. So far, the Who has been the road less travelled, if travelled at all, although the fruits to be harvested from so doing are the ones of a deeper, more robust and grounded leadership.

If virtual leaders want to be successful they have no choice but to take this road. By taking the detour of leading virtually, leaders will become better leaders; by becoming virtual leaders they will become *real* leaders.

In other words, if we want really to access the nature of effective virtual leadership, with all it brings in terms of newness, challenges and questions, we must have the courage and strength to become self-reflexive.

So what?

For now, I would like to invite you, my reader, to remember the following points when you lead virtually:

- Don't transfer into the virtual space what you have been doing in face-to-face situations

- Slow down and reflect on what you are experiencing when you lead virtually:

    o   What are you learning about yourself?

    o   What are you learning about others?

    o   When do you seem to connect well with others?

    o   Which aspects become critical?

- Be prepared to work hard at reflecting and learning. This might feel lonely at times because not so many have chosen this road so far. You might also want to get the help of a coach to practice self-reflexivity (you will find a list of questions to practice self-reflexivity in 'Tool Box H'.)

Final Considerations

My intention with this book has been to provide some practical help in the form of 'invitations', based on in-depth and robust reflection and research, that leaders can choose from and experiment with in order to learn and succeed in their virtual leadership. It will be up to readers to decide whether I have succeeded in this undertaking or not.

What this book cannot provide are conclusive statements about what it takes to lead effectively virtually because, as I have mentioned previously, much territory remains to be uncovered and much remains to be learnt.

This book is an invitation to try some practical experiments, which should lead to further reflection and on-going learning. It is a guide to help you becoming 'the virtual leader that you will become', and I wish you every success and luck in this endeavour.

Keep practising

I would like to complete this exploration of virtual leadership with the view of MilkCo's virtual leaders. Several among them underlined the need to keep practicing, hence emphasising the concept of virtual leadership as a new discipline:

"Now I think that we have learnt a lot, but I can forget. I need to continue using it"...

"You need to do this frequently in order to increase your efficiency. It is a new discipline that needs to be practised".

As you will have realised from the stories virtual leadership is not only a question of mindset and assumptions to be revisited. It is also a question of training and developing new skills (e.g. listening with your intuition). In other words it is about developing new muscles and, as in any sport, muscles need to keep active to strengthen and remain strong.

What you might be wondering about

Some readers might wonder why I did not include anything specifically addressing the challenge of working with multi-cultural groups in the virtual space. My research has shown that the cultural dimensions, for example the ones defined by Hofstede (see www.geert-hofstede.com) or Trompenaars & Hampden-Turner (1997), are not necessarily proving to be relevant in the virtual space. Different dimensions seem to become more significant: the use of silence (see Invitation 1) or the different ways in which 'trust' can be generated (see Matthew's story in Invitation 6).

From many years of practice I have learnt that it actually can be counter-productive to focus too much on the multi-cultural character of a group. Stereotyping people based on their national culture might be even more detrimental than in the face-to-face situation. Rather than focusing on the (national) cultural differences among team members, it is much more important in my experience to start with the *individuality* of each person and to understand each other's needs and preferences in the virtual space. For example the MBTI (Myers Briggs Type Indicator) profile of a team member might have as much of an impact on the way the person will behave in the virtual space as his/her culture.

A last story to think about ....

Finally I would like to tell you another true story and offer a further invitation. I was working with a young leader employed by one of the leading telecommunication giants, and I was asking him about his experience of leading virtually, as I knew that he had begun to transfer a lot of his activities into the virtual space.

Here is what he told me:

> "We had a few months to agree on and develop an implementation plan for this merger and here I was, in my cellar, in the middle of the night, working with the US and Asia, in my joggers and socks, my headset on, negotiating on one of the most important mergers for our company! My wife didn't want the kids to be disturbed as it was late at night and I might have woken them up by talking on the phone for so long, hence I had to go and work in the cellar with my rabbit as my only companion. It must have wondered what I was doing!"

Your days of impressive desks in representative offices, glamorous jet setting and stays in luxury hotels might be numbered ... how do you feel about that? How might this affect your sense of identity as a leader?

At least if you become an effective virtual leader you will be able to be much more choice-ful about when to travel the world and ... you might have more time available for inner travels as a result.

An invitation reminder

I would like to invite you to join me and to blog with me and with present and future readers of this book on the Black Gazelle website (**www.black-gazelle.com**). You are also welcome to contact me on **ghislaine.caulat@black-gazelle.com**

Please share your stories and learn from those of many others which you will find on the site as well. Let's expand the journey and make it a collective one with many, many more virtual leaders from all around the world.

I look forward to meeting you there!

Glossary

Action Research

Action Research is an approach to generating knowledge and combines different methods (such as reflection in groups, focus groups, interviews, personal reflection for example in the form of a journal). It is an interactive process combining the action with the reflection on this action. The assumption underlying this approach is that there is no learning (and knowledge) without action and that every action (if one takes the time to reflect on it) generates learning, and hence knowledge.

Action Research challenges traditional social science in the sense that it positions the generation of knowledge not as produced by experts who research, reflect on the knowledge available, express some hypothesis and test it with sampling actions but as a process of active moment-to-moment theorising, data collecting, and inquiry occurring in the midst of emergent structures. The knowledge is gained through action and for action.

For example Reason and Bradbury (2001) advocate that Action Research is about helping organisations and individuals to develop more practical knowledge and well being (economic, political, psychological and spiritual): they consider the purpose of Action Research as:

> "[...] to produce practical knowledge that is useful to people in the everyday conduct of their lives". (Idem, p.2)

McKernan (1996) shares this point of view; for him:

> "The aim of Action Research, as opposed to much traditional or fundamental research, is to solve the immediate and pressing day-to-day problems of practitioners". (Idem, p.3)

Asynchronous mode of working

See also 'synchronous mode of working'

Asynchronous work in the virtual space means that all people work in their own time (at a different time) and usually from different locations.

Examples of asynchronous work include:

- participating in a word-based online conference. All log on to a virtual platform where they can exchange written messages and join the debate in their own time. For example from a UK based time perspective it might be that one person logs in at 10.00 am, another at 7.00 pm, another at 11.00 pm, etc.; the conference and the exchange of views take place but stretched over a certain number of days

- participating in a blog (all log-in at the time they want but participate in the same conversation)

- Emails also represent a form of asynchronous work.

Asynchronous facilitation

Asynchronous facilitation relates to the facilitation of virtual events such as online conferences, online forums or blogs where the communication happens in the asynchronous mode. This facilitation is a genre in its own right and needs to be learnt as such. Facilitators need to understand how cognitive and emotional processes in asynchronous communication are different from the synchronous space. They need to develop the skills and competencies of working effectively with group dynamics taking into account the idiosyncrasies of the virtual asynchronous space. Unfortunately the need for these specific skills and competencies is often underestimated and asynchronous virtual events often do not succeed, not due to a lack of technological support but due to a lack of competence in terms of asynchronous facilitation.

Collaborative inquiry

Also known as 'cooperative inquiry' belongs to the same category of research approach as Action Research. It was first proposed by John Heron (1988) and later expanded with Peter Reason (1994).

Collaborative inquiry particularly underlines the fact that, to be valid, research in social science needs to happen 'with' rather than 'on' people. It emphasizes that all active participants are fully involved in research decisions and therefore all participants to the research become 'co-researchers'.

Cooperative inquiry creates a research cycle with four different types of knowledge: propositional knowing (the claims of knowledge and statements that we make based on the outcomes of our research), practical knowing (the knowledge that comes with actually doing what we propose), experiential knowing (the knowledge we receive in the actual moment of the interaction with our environment) and presentational knowing (the ways we choose to express and convey the knowledge that we have generated through our actions, in other words the way we choose to document our practice).

Phenomenology

Phenomenology as a discipline is related to other disciplines in philosophy, such as ontology (the study of being or what is) and epistemology (the study of knowledge) among others.

Phenomenology is a branch of (continental) European philosophy and was originally developed in the early 20th century in the works of Husserl. It was then further expanded by Heidegger, Sartre, Merleau-Ponty and others.

Literally, phenomenology is the study of 'phenomena': appearances of things, or things as they appear in our experience, or the ways we experience and perceive them, thus the meanings that we attribute to things based on our experience of these.

Phenomenology recognizes the subjective nature of knowledge and pays close attention to lived experience as a valid source of knowing. In this way it is distinctively different from most approaches which position the subject to study 'outside' of the researcher. For example when it comes to studying leadership, while traditional approaches would consist of studying it 'from the outside', as something to observe and reflect on according to certain rules of objectivity and validity, phenomenology underlines the subjectivity of our knowing and recognizes how the subjective world of the knower and his/her relationship to the object of his/her studies influences his/her knowing of the subject.

Reflective/reflexive

Reflection is understood to be a cognitive or intellectual activity, consisting of thinking about something in an objective, logical and neutral way, based on a realistic view of the world with a reality to be discovered, measured, categorized and properly explained.

Reflexivity on the other hand, is based on a social constructionist view of the world; in other words, there is no one single reality of the world – we shape our own social and organisational realities. Cunliffe (2009) explains:

> "[...] reflexivity goes deeper than reflection, because it means interrogating the taken-for-granted by questioning our relationship with our social world and the ways in which we account for our experience. [...] Managers as reflexive practitioners believe that we shape our social and organisational realities between us in our everyday interactions, and routinely engage in questioning this process".

A **self-reflexive** manager explores on a regular basis how (s)he IS in the world (as opposed to what he does), how he experiences and constructs his own identity/ies, the ones of others, his organisation and the world in general. (See Invitation 8, Figure 5 'Triple loop learning' and Tool Box H)

Social constructionism and social constructivism

Social constructionism and social constructivism are sociological theories of knowledge that consider how reality is socially constructed. They are about understanding how social reality and social phenomena get constructed and institutionalized. A social construction (social construct) is a concept or practice that is the construct (or artifact) of a particular group of people.

Social constructionism and social constructivism are related to each other but are also distinct. Social constructionism refers to the development of phenomena relative to social contexts while social constructivism refers to an individual's making meaning of knowledge within a given social context. Social constructionism can be described as a sociological concept whereas social constructivism can be described as a psychological concept.

The social constructionist view claims that humans in society create their worlds – 'Words make Worlds' – and so doing they also create themselves. Meaning is constantly created among ourselves and we have no choice but to create meaning, which requires making choices together (Gergen 1999). Moreover it claims that meaning can only be created in relationships: as individuals we are profoundly and solely social beings existing always and only in relationship with our world and with others.

Shotter (1993b) distinguishes 'knowing that' and 'knowing how' from a third kind of knowing. He refers to this as 'knowing from within' or 'joint action'. The first two kinds of knowing relate to the prescription of theories and causal succession, that is, 'words already spoken'. The third kind of knowing has to do with emergence, that is, 'words in their speaking'. In other terms, according to Shotter an essential part of knowing can only happen through the process of verbalising ideas which are then shaped in their meaning in contact with others as they listen and respond to these verbalised ideas.

The language is not seen any longer as a means of representing reality (a reality that exists out there); it is seen as shaping reality (because reality and we as human beings are intimately interwoven).

Our knowledge of the world depends on interactions between people, and the language becomes a process of sense-making between people.

This has important implications, namely that according to Shotter there is no such thing as 'inner thought':

> "[...] our thoughts, our self-consciously known thoughts, are not at first organised at the inner center of our being (in a nonmaterial 'soul', or a physiological 'lingua mentis') [...]. They only become organised, in a moment-by-moment, back-and-forth, formative or developmental process at the boundaries of our being". (Idem 1993, p.46)

Synchronous mode of working

See also 'asynchronous mode of working'

Synchronous work in the virtual space means that all people are working at the same time, albeit from different geographical places.

Examples of synchronous work include:

- having a teleconference with several people based in different locations
- having a web-based conference with several people based in different locations
- Having a video conference with people located in different places.

Traditional leading/working

In the context of my book, I use 'traditional leadership' to mean any leadership that occurs largely in the face-to-face mode, though clearly this does not exclude all phone calls, emails etc.

References

Alvesson, M 1996, "Leadership Studies: from procedure and abstraction to reflexivity and situation", *Leadership Quarterly*, vol. 7, no. 4, pp.455-485.

Argyris, C & Schön, D 1996, *Organisational learning II: Theory, method and practice*, Addison Wesley, Reading Mass.

Bandler, R & Grinder, J 1979, *Frogs into Princes: Neuro Linguistic Programming*, Real People Press, Moab UT.

Bell, S B & Kozlowski, S W 2002, "A Typology of Virtual Teams. Implications for Effective Leadership", *Group & Organization Management*, vol. 27, no. 1, pp.14-29.

Berendt, J E 2007, *Nada Brahma. Die Welt ist Klang*, Suhrkamp Verlag, Frankfurt-am-Main.

Binney, G, Wilke, G & Williams, C 2005, *Living Leadership A Practical Guide for Ordinary Heroes*, FT Prentice Hall.

Caldwell, C 2004, "Launching virtual remote teams", *China Staff*, Hong Kong, vol. 10, no. 9, pp.27-30.

Carroll, J, Howard S, Vetere F, Peck J & Murphy J 2001 "Identity, Power And Fragmentation in Cyberspace: Technology Appropriation by Young People" *ACIS 2001 Proceedings*, Paper 6.

Caulat, G 2004, "Be heard but not seen", Ashridge Master in Organisation Consulting (AMOC) thesis, Ashridge Business School.

Cheng B S, Chou LF, Wu T Y, Huang M P & Farh J L 2004, "Paternalistic leadership and subordinate responses: Establishing a leadership model in Chinese organizations" *Asian Journal of Social Psychology*, no. 7, pp.89-117.

Cunliffe, A L 2009b, "The Philosopher Leader: On Relationism, Ethics and Reflexivity. A Critical Perspective to Teaching Leadership", *Management Learning*, vol. 40; no. 87.

Foulkes, S H 1975, *Group analytic psychotherapy, method and principles*, Gordon & Breach, London.

Furst, S A, Reeves, M, Rosen, B & Blackburn, R S 2004, "Managing the life cycle of virtual teams", *Academy of Management Executive*, vol. 18, no. 2, pp.6-22.

Gergen, K J 1999, *An invitation to Social Construction*, Sage, London.

Gilligan, C, Spencer R, Weinberg K M & Bertsch T 2006, "On the Listening Guide. A Voice-Centered Relational Method" in S N Hesse-Biber (ed.), *Emergent Methods in Social Research*, Sage, London.

Golden, T D & Veiga, J F 2008, "The impact of superior – subordinate relationships on the commitment, job satisfaction, and performance of virtual workers", *The Leadership Quarterly* 19, pp.77-88.

Griffin, D 2002, *The Emergence of Leadership. Linking Self-Organising and Ethics*, Routledge, London & New York.

Handy, C 1995, "Trust and the virtual organization", *Harvard Business Review*, vol. 73, no. 3, pp.40-50.

Heron J (1988) see Reason P (ed) 1988

Heron, J 1999, *The Complete Facilitator's Handbook*, Kogan Page, London.

Hine, C 2000, *Virtual Ethnography*, Sage Publications, London.

Hofstede, G see http://www.geert-hofstede.com

Isaacs, W 1999, *Dialogue and the Art of Thinking Together*, Currency, New York.

Jarvenpaa, S L & Leidner, D E 1999, "Communication and Trust in Global Virtual Teams", *Organization Science* vol. 10, no. 6, pp.791-815.

Joshi, A, Lazarova M B & Liao H 2009, "Getting everyone on Board: The Role of Inspirational Leadership in Geographically Dispersed Teams", *Organization Science*, vol. 20, no. 1, January-February, pp.240-252.

Katzenbach, J R & Smith, D K 1993, *The Wisdom of Teams: Creating the High Performance Organization*, Harvard Business School, Boston MA.

Kirkman, B L, Rosen, B, Tesluk, P E & Gibson, C B & McPherson, S O 2002, " Five challenges to virtual team success: Lessons from Sabre, Inc", *Academy of Management Executive*, vol. 16, no. 3, pp.67-79.

Ladkin, D 2010, *Rethinking Leadership. A new look at old leadership questions*, Edward Elgar Publishing, Cheltenham UK.

Lakoff, G & Johnson, M 1999, *Philosophy in the Flesh. The Embodied Mind and Its Challenge to Western Thought*, Basic Books.

Lipnack, J & Stamps, J 1997, *Virtual Teams: reaching across space, time, and organizations with technology*, John Wiley & Sons, London.

Luhmann, N 1973, *Vertrauen. Ein Mechanismus der Reduktion sozialer Komplexität*, Ferdinand Enke Verlag, Stuttgart.

McKernan, J 1996, *Curriculum Action Research*, 2nd Edition, Kogan Page.

Mehrabian, A 1971, *Silent Messages: Implicit Communication of Emotions and Attitudes*, Wadsworth Publishing Company.

Meyerson, D, Weick, K E & Kramer, R M 1996 "Swift trust and temporary groups" in RM Kramer & TR Tyler (eds), *Trust in organisations: Frontiers of theory and research*, Sage, Thousand Oaks, CA, pp.166-195.

Myers, Isabel, Briggs, Katharine; McCauley Mary H.; Quenk, Naomi L.; Hammer, Allen L. (1998). *MBTI Manual (A guide to the development and use of the Myers Briggs type indicator)*. Consulting Psychologists Press; 3rd edition.

Myers Briggs Type Indicator Foundation http://www.myersbriggs.org/my-mbti-personality-type/mbti-basics/

Nevis, E C 2001, *Organizational Consulting, A Gestalt Approach*, Gestalt Press, London.

O'Hara-Devereaux, M & Johansen, R 1994, *Globalwork*, Jossey-Bass, San Francisco, CA.

Oshri, I, Kotlarsky J & Willcocks L 2008, "Socialisation in a global context: Lessons from dispersed teams" in N Panteli & M Chiasson (eds) *Exploring Virtuality within and beyond organizations*, Palgrave, pp.21-54.

Panteli, N 2005 "Trust in global virtual teams", *Ariadne*, no. 43, Originating URL: http://www.ariadne.ac.uk/ issue 43/panteli/intro.htlm (no page number available).

Panteli, N & Chiasson, M 2008, *Exploring virtuality within and beyond organizations. Social Global and Local Dimensions*, Palgrave Macmillan.

Panteli, N & Fineman, S, 2006 "The Sound of Silence: the case of virtual team organising" in *Behaviour and Information Technology*. vol. 24, no. 5, pp. 347-352.

Perls, F S 1969, *Gestalt Therapy Verbatim, The Gestalt Journal*, 16-4.

Peschl, M F 2007, "Triple-loop learning as foundation for profound change, individual cultivation, and radical innovation. Construction processes beyond scientific and rational knowledge", *Constructivist Foundations*, vol. 2 (2-3), pp.136–145.

Prensky, M 2001a, "Digital Natives, Digital Immigrants", *On the Horizon*, MCB University Press, vol. 9 no. 5.

Prensky, M 2001b, "Digital Natives, Digital Immigrants, Part II: Do they really *think* differently", *On the Horizon*, MCB University Press, vol. 9 no. 6.

Reason, P (ed) 1988 *"Human inquiry in action"* Sage, incl J Heron *"Impressions of the other reality"*.

Reason, P 1994, "Three approaches to participatory inquiry" in N Denzin & Y Lincoln (eds), *Handbook of Qualitative Research*, Sage Publications, London.

Reason, P & Bradbury, H 2001, "Introduction: Inquiry and Participation in Search of a World Worthy of Human Aspiration" in Reason, P & Bradbury, H (eds), *Handbook of Action Research*. Sage Publications, London, pp.1-14.

Remdisch S & Utsch A 2006, "Führen auf Distanz. Neue Herausforderungen für Organisation und Management", *OrganisationsEntwicklung*, vol. 3, pp.32-43.

Rymaszenski, M, Au, W J, Winters, C, Onndrejka, C & Cunningham, B 2007, *Second Life: The Official Guide*, John Wiley, New Jersey.

Senge, Peter M, Scharmer, C Otto, Jaworski, Joseph and Flowers, Betty-Sue 2005 *Presence: An Exploration of Profound Change in People, Organizations, and Society*, Doubleday NY.

Scharmer, C Otto, 2007 *Theory U: Leading from the Future as it Emerges*, Society for Organizational Learning, Cambridge, MA.

Shotter, J 1993, *Cultural Politics of Everyday Life: Social Constructionism, Rhetoric, and Knowing of the Third Kind*, Open University Press, Milton Keynes.

Stacey, R 1992, *Managing the Unknowable: Strategic Boundaries Between Order and Chaos in Organizations*, CA Jossey-Bass Publishers, San Francisco.

Stacey, R & Griffin, D (eds) 2005, *A Complexity Perspective on Researching Organisations*, Routledge, New York.

Starr, A & Torbert B 2005, "Timely and Transforming Leadership Inquiry and Action: Toward Triple-loop Awareness", *Integral Review* 1, pp.85-97.

Suler, J (no date, a), 'Presence in Cyberspace', viewed on 20/10/07 on www.rider.edu/ suler/psycyber/psycyber.html.

Trompenaars, Fons & Hampden-Turner, Charles 1997, *Riding the Waves of Culture: Understanding Diversity in Global Business*. (Second Edition) London: Nicholas Brealey

Wasson, C 2004, "Multitasking During Virtual Meetings", *Human Resource Planning*, vol. 27, pp.47-60.

Wilber, K 2001, *A Theory of Everything*, Shambhala, Boston.

Williams, V 2002, *Virtual Leadership*, Shadowbrook Publishing, Edison, New Jersey.

Wilson, J M, Strauss, S G & Evily, B 2006 "All in due time: the development of Trust in computer-mediated and face-to-face teams", *Organizational Behavior and Human Decision Processes* 99, pp.16-33.

Woolgar, S 1991a, "Configuring the user: the case of usability trials" in J Law (ed.), *A Sociology of Monsters: Essays on Power, Technology and Domination*, Routledge, pp.57-98.

Woolgar, S 1991b, "The Turn to Technology in Social Studies of Science", *Science, Technology & Human Values: Journal of the society for social studies of science*, vol. 16, PT1, pp.20-49.

Yoo, Y & Alavi, M 2003, "Emergent leadership in virtual teams: what do emergent leaders do?" *Information and Organization* 14, pp.27-58.

Zhang, S & Fjermestad, J 2006, "Bridging the gap between traditional leadership theories and virtual team leadership", *Int. J. Technology, Policy and Management*, vol. 6, no.3, pp.275-291.

Appendix

An Introduction to My Key Fellow Researchers

(In order to protect the identity of my co-researchers I have changed their names and those of their companies. I do so with all managers and companies throughout this book.)

William is a Belgian manager at a senior level in CompCorp. He has led teams (approximately 1,500 people in total) over six plants in Belgium and Sweden in a blend of face-to-face and virtual work for the last three years. I got to know William during a leadership development programme which was run by Ashridge Consulting. I soon developed a strong respect for William, in particular for his attitude, which I felt was open, thoughtful and engaging. During the time that I worked with him, William had to overcome extremely challenging situations in terms of management and leadership, and the need for him to lead virtually became ever more critical.

Sten is British and works for a multinational process engineering company. At the time of my research Sten was in charge of a particular market segment in the Nordic and Baltic countries and the UK. He was responsible for a virtual team including five direct reports based in different countries and another seven indirect reports in other countries. He was based in the UK while his boss was based in Finland. I had known Sten for at least ten years. I got to know him when I was working at RolloCorp and we did a lot of work together. Sten and I got on well and, as with William, I have always appreciated his openness. My work with Sten stopped earlier than that with William and Silvia because, after about a year, Sten changed his role to local Sales Director, still within the same organisation, but without the regular need to work virtually.

Silvia represents a different case. I have never met her face-to-face. I only got to know her within the context of my research. She was recommended by a friend and immediately agreed to participate in the research. Silvia is German and works in Sweden for a global telecommunication company: she leads a team across the world (Japan, China, Korea, US, Brazil, Mexico,

Hungary and Sweden). Silvia's is a typical matrix-based team, which means that she has no direct reports. At the time I started working with Silvia the team had met face-to-face only twice in three years.

Some way into my research, I organised and facilitated a collaborative inquiry with three virtual leaders, all based in different organisations. This proved to be a very rewarding and rich experience as well. The people engaged in this inquiry were:

Matthew, who was working globally as an accounting director for an IT company

Barbara, the CEO of an NGO working across geographical zones including India, Africa and the UK

Silvia, who was mentioned earlier as one of the leaders I had been accompanying over the previous two years on a one-to-one basis.

None of the three inquirers knew each other before our work together and they did not meet face-to-face during the process.

I also introduce **MilkCo**, a global organisation with whom I have worked virtually on a major strategy project. I refer to this assignment throughout the text as it occurs at the junction of my research and my consulting, and provides a wealth of useful insights.

The Virtual Leadership Tool Box

In this section you will find a series of carefully selected tools of different sorts and shapes which might be helpful in your virtual leadership role.

This tool box is really meant as a 'box': it is there to help yourself to the tools that you will find most useful. Feel free to experiment with the tools appealing to you and to discard the others.

I would be delighted if you shared your experience of using the tools with the other readers of the book. Please see details on how to join the learning community on virtual leadership at the end of 'Final Considerations' (see page 127).

A. Summary of Hygiene Principles for Synchronous Virtual Meetings (e.g. Teleconferences and Web-conferences)

1.   All meeting participants should be linked in virtually – **There should be no mix of people sitting face-to-face with people linked in virtually.**

2.   Participants should all be in a **quiet room**, alone and undisturbed (no session from the car, the train, the airline lounge, the open plan office, etc.).

3.   Participants should be equipped with a **headset covering both ears**. I recommend using telephony (no computer-based lines) because of a better quality and availability of lines.

4.   Participants' phones should be equipped with a **battery that is sufficiently strong** to last the whole duration of the meeting. People often forget about this and get disconnected during the meeting, which can become pretty disruptive for all involved.

5.   Participants should be invited to **log-in ten to five minutes before the official start** of the meeting (depending on the complexity of the technology used) so that last minute technical problems can be sorted in time for a prompt start. If you use bespoke technology for the first time with the participants, do plan a separate trial call (or technical test) of ten minutes a few days prior to the meeting. This will help to avoid bad surprises and the participant will feel more confident at the start of the meeting.

6.   I recommend the use of a **'focus exercise'** (see Tool Box C) at the start of the meeting to enable participants to switch off their current preoccupations and 'tune-into' the virtual meeting.

7.   Plan sufficient time at the start of the meeting for everybody to connect well with each other at a personal and emotional level before diving into the task. Apply the principle of **'getting everybody's voice into the virtual space'** before starting the discussion on the task. At the end of the meeting do practice a **'disconnecting ritual'** where everybody is asked to say a few words before leaving the meeting as a way to disconnect at a personal level. This is the virtual 'hand shake'.

8.   During the meeting make sure that you take **sufficient breaks**: virtual meetings can be perceived (at least for people not used to it) as very tiring. Do discuss with the participants to the meeting how often to take breaks and for how long.

9. Plan a **buffer before and after the virtual meeting**. Give yourself some time to get ready for the meeting and some time to complete mentally and emotionally with the virtual meeting before moving on to the next meeting.

10. Make sure that at the time of the meeting you are not hungry, not thirsty, not tired, not too hot or cold.

11. Be aware that if you are nervous, anxious, under pressure, etc. these feelings and emotions will get amplified in the virtual space. If you can't avoid having these, then be explicit about these at the start of the meeting and create an atmosphere that enables other attendees to do the same.

12. Invite the other attendees to apply the same principles (9, 10 and 11).

B. Further Hints and Tips for Your Synchronous Meetings

A. If you plan for a meeting (e.g. a web-based meeting) where complex decisions or innovative or strategic thinking are required I recommend the three following roles:

- **One person leading the meeting** (usually the team leader) although you might decide to rotate the leadership

- **One person facilitating the meeting** and paying particular attention to the process and the team's dynamics, taking into account the idiosyncrasies of the virtual space

- **One technical facilitator** dedicated to ensuring a smooth running of the meeting with as few technical hurdles as possible.

B. Work actively on the dimension asynchronous – synchronous: this means that you need to plan beforehand what can be done asynchronously (i.e. read and/or prepared by people in their own time before the meeting) as opposed to what needs to be done synchronously (by all together at the same time).

C. Be clear about the communication milestones (when to send the invitation, when to send the agenda, when to send a reminder, etc.). There is no specific rule regarding the exact timings of this as this depends on the company's culture and team's activities.

D. Don't underestimate the importance of reminders.

E. I recommend that you ask people for feedback on the agenda when you send it out and that you give them a deadline for this feedback: this will increase buy-in and commitment.

F. Plan how you will document discussion outcomes – I highly recommend online simultaneous minutes as this is a very powerful way of consolidating understanding, raising engagement and commitment.

G. When fixing the time for the meeting, if you work across time zones, produce a scheduling table to become aware of the different timings involved and avoid asking people to get up in the middle of the night for your meeting (see example in Tool Box D).

H. When preparing for your web-based meeting, consider producing two types of material:

- A plan for the meeting: I mean here much more than the agenda sent to the attendees. I mean a plan with key steps, key activities, contents and timings.

- The slides for the meeting: prepare not only content slides but also process slides (for example have one slide ready with some questions on it to encourage people to connect with each other, or have one slide with a specific question to encourage the group to reflect or give feedback on something).

- Avoid presentations that are longer than 10 minutes (most people tend to disengage if a monologue is longer than 3–4 minutes in the virtual space). Please consider what can be sent in advance as pre-reading.

C. Focus Exercise

Short history of this exercise

In the context of my inquiry and experimentation with the virtual facilitation of action learning, the several experiments that I did with clients led me to realise the importance of being well aware of one's body and bodily sensations when doing virtual work. The reason for this is to avoid the projection of one's own feelings and emotions on to others in the virtual space, and/or the psychological phenomenon of 'confluence' where one gets into a kind of symbiosis with somebody else in the virtual space, making it impossible to distinguish between the two worlds (my world and the world of the other) any longer. In order to help my clients in the virtual world to be as grounded as possible and enter into a 'healthy' connection with others in the virtual space, I developed a so-called focus exercise and decided to make it an integral part of most of my virtual interventions.

Participants tend to find it weird at the beginning but, in the vast majority of the cases, soon come to the conclusion that it is a very useful way of 'tuning into' the virtual meeting and connecting with others in the virtual space.

I highly recommend this practice as it makes a significant difference to the quality of the connectivity between people. Should you however feel that this is too big a leap for you to lead your team members or the meeting participants through such an exercise, I recommend that you at least do the exercise for yourself (on your own) before the meeting.

Example of a focus exercise: Example 1

Close your eyes

Breathe deeply in and out, deeply in and out...

Imagine that you are a small laser travelling through your body

As a small laser you explore your body

You start with your feet

You feel the ground under your feet

You go into your toes, one toe after the other one

You notice any sensation or tension in your toes

Notice any sensation or tension in your heels

Slowly you go up your leg, up to your knees

Slowly go further up your thighs

Notice any sensations, any feelings in your legs

You breathe deeply in and out, deeply in and out...

You now go into your bottom

You feel your bottom on the seat: is your seat hard, soft, warm, cold...?

You notice any sensation in your bottom

You now explore the lower part of your belly and of your back

You go up to your stomach

You go up along your spine

Notice the rhythm of your breathing

Notice any sensation in your stomach

Notice any tension along your spine

You now go further up to your chest

You breathe deeply and slowly in and out, in and out...

Notice any sensations in your chest

You now go into your shoulders, your neck

If you feel any tensions, in your mind, blow warm air into the tensions

You now explore your face, your chin, your cheeks

You explore your eyes, your forehead

Notice any sensations behind your eyes

Notice any sensation in your forehead

Breathe deeply in and out, deeply in and out...

You now explore your head; you explore the cavity of your head

Notice any sensation, any tension, any noise...

You notice the thoughts coming into your mind

You let them come and go again, come and go again...

You imagine a fresh breeze on your forehead

You feel fresh, relaxed, fully alert

Breathe deeply in and out, deeply in and out...

You now sense the presence of your colleagues in this virtual meeting

You will think of each colleague, one after the other, including yourself

You start focusing your mind on X (name one of the participants to the meeting)

You remember her voice, the tone of her voice

You remember what she said last time you talked to her

If you don't remember what she said, just feel her presence now

You breathe deeply in and out, deeply in and out...

You now focus on Y (name of another participant to the meeting)

[Repeat the above]

[Finish with yourself as facilitator/meeting leader as follows:]

You now focus on Z (the facilitator/leader)

You listen to her/his voice, the tone of her/his voice

Just feel her/his presence now

You now think of yourself again in this space

Notice how you feel, notice the thoughts coming and going [short pause]

Breathe in and out, deeply and slowly, in and out...

Just stay there for a little while [pause]

Now at your own pace, open your eyes

When you are ready, say your name and 'I am ready for the meeting'.

Example of a focus exercise: Example 2 (lighter version)

Close your eyes

Check the position of your body on the chair (or seat) and make sure that you sit comfortably

Start paying attention to your breathing: pay attention to the pace and the depth of your breathing

Regulate it in a way that with every intake of air you come into closer connection with your body

Breathing in and out.... (repeat two or three times)

Become aware of the point of contact between your feet and the ground: press the soles of your feet against the ground to clearly feel it under your feet

Become aware of the whole weight of your body on the chair: feel the point of contact between your bottom and the seat.

Become aware of your face: become aware of any tension or contraction there. Smile to yourself and relax your face.

Become aware of what is going on for you right now: are you sensing, feeling or thinking?

If you are sensing, what is it you are sensing?

If you are feeling, what is it you are feeling?

If you are thinking, what are your thoughts? Try to identify the thoughts related to this meeting and the ones that have nothing to do with it.

Try to park the latter the best way you can and let them go...

If they come back, acknowledge them and let them go again

You now sense the presence of your colleagues in this virtual meeting

You will think of each colleague, one after the other, including yourself

You start focusing your mind on X (name one of the participants to the meeting)

Just feel his/her presence now

You breathe deeply in and out, deeply in and out...

You now focus on Y (name of another participant to the meeting)

[Repeat the above]

[Finish with yourself as facilitator/meeting leader as follows:]

You now focus on Z (the facilitator/leader)

Just feel her/his presence now

You now think of yourself again in this space

Notice how you feel, notice the thoughts coming and going [short pause]

Breathe in and out, deeply and slowly, in and out...

Just stay there for a little while [pause]

Now in your own time, open your eyes

When you are ready, say your name and 'I am ready for the meeting'.

D. Scheduling Virtual Synchronous Meetings

The scheduling list on page 150 is a simple device to identify the most accept-able time for synchronous virtual meetings when you work with people scattered around the globe. In some instances it will not be possible to find times that are 'normal' day times for all involved, simply because of the lack of compatibility of the time zones involved. In this case it will help to rotate the difficult timings between the meetings so that the same people do not always have to get up at 3.00 am in the morning. This is the **principle of 'sharing the pain':** in my experience this makes a big difference to the trust in the virtual team as everybody feels respected with their needs and differ-ences. It is also a clear signal against headquarters-centric thinking: when most people attending the meeting are based let's say in Frankfurt (Germany) it seems the most obvious to have a meeting at 10.00 am German time and to forget individual participants' timing based for example in Beijing or Detroit.

Using this device it is not only important to identify the best possible timing for all involved, the biggest value is actually in the open discussion about scheduling the virtual meetings: the open discussion with the team based on the table overleaf where all can see the implications for a selected timing for everybody is the most valuable part. All take the time to agree on the best timing, taking each other's specific situation and needs into consid-eration and in an open and transparent way. This might feel like a significant amount of time investment at the beginning (if the table is well prepared, it should not take more than 15 minutes), however, once the best timings and principles have been discussed, the scheduling will subsequently become a natural process and be part of your virtual team culture.

Row number	Chicago	NL/CH	Shanghai	Sydney
1	01.00	08.00	15.00	17.00
2	02.00	09.00	16.00	18.00
3	03.00	10.00	17.00	19.00
4	04.00	11.00	18.00	20.00
5	05.00	12.00	19.00	21.00
6	06.00	13.00	20.00	22.00
7	07.00	14.00	21.00	23.00
8	08.00	15.00	22.00	24.00
9	09.00	16.00	23.00	01.00
10	10.00	17.00	24.00	02.00
11	11.00	18.00	01.00	03.00
12	12.00	19.00	02.00	04.00
13	13.00	20.00	03.00	05.00
14	14.00	21.00	04.00	06.00
15	15.00	22.00	05.00	07.00
16	16.00	23.00	06.00	08.00
17	17.00	24.00	07.00	09.00
18	18.00	01.00	08.00	10.00
19	19.00	02.00	09.00	11.00
20	20.00	03.00	10.00	12.00
21	21.00	04.00	11.00	13.00
22	22.00	05.00	12.00	14.00
23	23.00	06.00	13.00	15.00
24	24.00	07.00	14.00	16.00

While this table (intentionally illustrating a rather difficult combination of time zones) suggests least desirable times (dark grey shading) and less desirable times to start meetings (light grey), these definitions of least and less desirable would, initially, need to be checked to take account of different cultures and personal preferences. It will also be a helpful device to decide on the principle of 'sharing the pain'.

E. Designing Communication

The table below is meant as a guide to help you selecting the communication technology for specific purposes.

Purpose of virtual intervention	Critical aspects to bear in mind	Suggested communication technology
Making sense of information	This work can be done asynchronously as long as information is well prepared. In some instances some synchronous work will be very helpful to strengthen feeling of shared understanding and togetherness.	Asynchronous exchange for example on Sharepoint (a web application platform developed by Microsoft. It allows among other things for document and file management, collaboration spaces, social networking tools, etc.) A teleconference in addition to the asynchronous exchange might be very beneficial.
Exploring work outcomes	This work can be done asynchronously as long as information is well prepared and next steps or questions to reflect on are clearly specified.	Asynchronous exchange for example using a blog to share, compare and contrast individual views. A web-based word only based conference with dedicated facilitation can also be very useful.
Updating each other	This work can be done asynchronously as long as information is well prepared. In some instances some synchronous work will be very helpful to strengthen feeling of togetherness.	Asynchronous exchange for example on Sharepoint (see above). A teleconference in addition to the asynchronous exchange might be very beneficial.
Developing strategies and action plans Making complex decisions	The synchronous element in the communication is highly critical here. While information might be exchanged asynchronously prior to the virtual meeting, it is very important for all parties to actually come together at the same time and discuss what needs to happen.	A synchronous web-based meeting (using telephony for the audio and web-based document exchange) so that all can co-create documents and reflect together. Use of cameras is not necessary! Examples of platforms are WebEx, LifeMeeting, GoToMeeting, NetMeeting, Interwise, etc.

Purpose of virtual intervention	Critical aspects to bear in mind	Suggested communication technology
Brainstorming	This work can be done asynchronously as long as information is well prepared. In some instances some synchronous work will be very helpful to strengthen feeling of togetherness.	Asynchronous exchange for example using a blog to share, compare and contrast individual views. A web-based word only based conference with dedicated facilitation can also be very useful. In this case there is big value in the asynchronous element as the process slows down and enables people to think about things from different perspectives by reading other people's views on the blog or web-based word only conference. The process needs to be well facilitated though – like any innovative process –and requires virtual asynchronous facilitation (see glossary) skills.
Resolving conflict	The synchronous element of the conversation is absolutely essential here! It is important to take the conversation step-by-step: first on a one-to-one basis, then on a group basis, if relevant. People should be in the right environment for this (quiet, alone, focused) and it might be necessary to schedule the call properly.	One-to-one phone calls (no email!) followed by Teleconference (if several people are involved in the conflict).
Informal exchange – The virtual coffee machine conversation	The synchronous element of the communication is not to be underestimated. Visuals are not necessarily critical for this, depending on what you want to achieve.	A teleconference setting might suffice. However in some instances a web-based platform might be helpful, for example to share podcasts, pictures, pieces of music, etc.

F. The Foundation of High Performance in the Virtual Team

A few questions to get your virtual team started on a robust basis

Sharing Understanding
- What is our team's purpose?
- What are our goals?
- What are our deliverables?
- What is my role: why am I important to the team?
- What's in it for me?

Agreeing ways of working virtually
- What do we need to do synchronously?
- What will we do asynchronously?
- What are the 'workable' time windows for us?
- When will we have our teleconferences or web meetings?
- How will we take decisions virtually?
- When do we all need to be involved?
- What is an acceptable response time for us?
- What other rules and protocols do we need?

Trust in our team
- What is the level of diversity in our team? How many cultures are represented? How different are our personalities?
- How much trust already exists in the team? What can we amplify? How?
- What might get in the way of our virtual cooperation?
- What could be potential conflicts of interests?
- What other types of conflicts might arise?
- How will we handle conflicts virtually?

Communication
- What communication technology is available to us?
- How proficient are we with this technology?
- What do we need to learn?
- When do we want to use which technology for what? (see Tool Box E)
- What should be our email protocol?
- How do we want to represent ourselves and communicate outside our team?
- How and where will we create, update and save documents?

You might want to use the four categories of questions to develop your team charter.

The value of the discussion of these questions in the team is just as important as the charter!

The charter would need to be reviewed regularly:
- What are we learning as a virtual team?
- What works well? What can be improved?
- What do we want to do differently? Where do we need to amend our charter?

G. Helping You to Slow Down for Effective Virtual Leadership

I observe on a regular basis that managers tend to squeeze virtual meetings in between face-to-face meetings as they do not need to travel anywhere for the former ones. Often meetings (e.g. teleconferences, web-meetings) are scheduled on the minute after the previous meeting and up until the minute of the start of the next one. No buffer is planned and the rhythm of work seems to accelerate exponentially. However rhythm of meetings does not equate to productivity. Paradoxically, as we can see from the stories in this book, effective work in the virtual space means first of all *slowing down*.

Here are **eight reminders of how to slow down** in the virtual space:

1. Plan buffers of time before and after virtual synchronous meetings (see Tool Box A)

2. Take the time to prepare well for your synchronous meetings and ask other attendees to do the same (see Invitation 5)

3. Focus exercise (see Tool Box C)

4. Take the time at the beginning of the synchronous meeting to build the emotional and cognitive connection among attendees before jumping to the work contents. Apply the principle of **getting everybody's voice** in the space (see Tool Box A)

5. Listen well using your intuition (see Invitation 2)

6. Learn to work with silences (see Invitation 1)

7. Take the time to close the emotional and cognitive connection among attendees before closing the meeting (see Tool Box A)

8. Take the time to reflect on your leadership in the virtual space in between synchronous virtual meetings (see Tool Box F and H)

H. Questions to Exercise Reflexivity in Virtual Leadership

The following list of questions is meant to help you to reflect on a regular basis on the way you lead virtually. It aims to help you to develop a clear virtual leadership profile and become 'the virtual leader that you will become'.

When have you been at your best when leading virtually in the last two to three weeks?
- What did you do?
- What did you say?
- Who were you with?
- What does this tell you about your virtual leadership?
- How do you feel about that?

How would you define your identity as a virtual leader?
- How do you think you come across to others in the virtual space?
- What does your voice convey about you? What would you like it to convey?
- What does your behaviour in the virtual space convey about you? What would you like it to convey?

What do you still find challenging when it comes to leading and working virtually?
- Why is it like that?
- Is there anything you need to learn in this respect?
- Any assumptions that you find difficult to revisit?
- Anything you find difficult to change in your mindset or behaviour?
- What would it take for you to change this?
- How much do you want to change it?

How leader-full have you been when trying to change and/or help others to change?

- What compromises have you made?

- Have these been helpful and in what way?

- When did these compromises get in the way of effective virtual working?

- Why?

- What does this mean for next time?

How much time and effort do you spend building and nurturing relationships in the virtual space?

- How much time do you plan to spend on this during the virtual meetings?

- How much time do you spend and which activities do you undertake to build relationships in-between virtual meetings?

How much trust do you feel currently exists in your virtual team?

- When do you feel most trustful?

- When do you feel most trusted?

- Is there anything else you could do to increase the trust?

- What is currently getting in the way of trust?

- What can you do about that?

What are your own personal sources of power in the virtual space?

- How do you know that you are powerful in these moments?

- What can you do to amplify these moments?

- What can you do to help others to find their power in the virtual space?

Index

action learning ix, 18, 43, 84
- virtual action learning 37, 42, 76, 78, 95, 144
action research 14, 128, 129
agenda 28, 30, 58, 59, 62, 64, 65, 73, 74, 91, 92, 142
amplification 27, 30, 31, 32, 34, 88, 97, 120, 141, 153, 156
Ashridge 16, 19–21, 41, 72, 103
asynchronous 34, 70–1, 82, 106–7, 129, 132, 142, 151–3
- facilitation 70–1, 129, 152
attachment 18, 39
attention 17, 19, 31, 32, 47, 50, 55, 60, 61, 63, 75, 89, 93, 99, 101, 121, 122, 147
- span 52
auditory preference 43
authority
- earned 87
- figures 44
awareness 9, 29, 31, 33, 38, 50, 66, 81, 93, 120–1
- levels of 21, 120, 123

background noise 34
bad habits 33, 35, 36
'being' 9, 117, 119, 120, 130, 132
best practice 78
blogging 34, 105, 127, 129, 151, 152
body language 37, 39, 42–3, 60, 92, 96, 105
boundaries 49, 80, 83, 88, 120, 132

chat room 38, 47, 49, 69, 109
Cisco 39
closure 53
coaching 19–20, 29, 31, 38, 65, 66, 72, 79, 106
collaborative inquiry 17–18, 73, 79, 83, 86, 87, 88, 93, 95, 99, 129, 138
collective 18, 38, 107, 109, 123, 127
common interest 94–5
communication 8, 24, 25, 27, 30, 35, 43, 48, 61, 69, 76, 78–80, 90, 101, 103, 105, 106–9, 111, 119, 129
- design 107
- non-verbal 43
competencies 14, 63, 80–1, 107, 129
concentration 28, 33, 50, 65
conflicts 106–7, 153
connecting ix, 22, 40, 43, 52, 53, 54, 89, 106, 119, 144
conscious choice 36, 63, 100, 109
consensus 72, 85
control 47–8, 50, 52, 54, 99, 101–2, 103
corridor meetings 56, 59, 62
counter-intuitive 4, 54
cyberspace 23, 50, 56, 62, 110

dialogue 9, 18, 30, 100, 109
Digital Natives 23–4, 51–2, 96–7, 104
discipline 6, 8, 27–9, 36, 40, 44, 57, 125, 130

emotions ix, 28, 31–2, 36, 41, 45, 68, 141, 144
- field 119
- glue 60, 89
energy levels 57, 85, 93
engaging 13, 16, 27, 36, 44, 49, 54, 137
event-based 82
existential 120–1
expectations 62, 72, 86, 102
experiential learning 21
experiment vii, 1, 5, 11, 28, 29, 32, 43, 45, 54, 76, 77, 79, 82, 89, 117–19, 123, 125, 139, 144
expertise 76, 78, 85, 97–9, 101
eye contact 39, 96

Facebook 23, 25, 104–5
facilitation 20, 68, 70, 74–5, 80–1, 106, 129, 144, 151, 152
feelings 27–9, 41, 43–5, 57, 85, 95, 141, 144
focus ix, 8, 9, 27–9, 31, 38, 39, 48, 50, 61, 65–8, 77, 85, 113, 121, 126
focus exercise 28–9, 85, 140, 144–8, 154
follow-up 59